LYRIC POETRY AS STATE CRITICISM IN MODERN JAPAN

LYRIC POETRY AS STATE CRITICISM IN MODERN JAPAN

Marianne Tarcov

CORNELL EAST ASIA SERIES
An imprint of
CORNELL UNIVERSITY PRESS
Ithaca and London

Number 227 in the Cornell East Asia Series

Copyright © 2026 by Cornell University

All rights reserved. Except for brief quotations in a review, this book, or parts thereof, must not be reproduced in any form without permission in writing from the publisher. For information, address Cornell University Press, Sage House, 512 East State Street, Ithaca, New York 14850. Visit our website at cornellpress.cornell.edu.

First published 2026 by Cornell University Press

Librarians: A CIP catalog record for this book is available from the Library of Congress.

ISBN 978-1-5017-8602-0 (hardcover)
ISBN 978-1-5017-8678-5 (paperback)
ISBN 978-1-5017-8603-7 (pdf)
ISBN 978-1-5017-8604-4 (epub)

GPSR EU contact: Sam Thornton, Mare Nostrum Group B.V., Mauritskade 21D, 1091 GC, Amsterdam, NL, gpsr@mare-nostrum.co.uk.

Contents

Introduction: The Politics of Lyric and the Poetry of Officially Licensed State Critique   1

1. Critiquing Meiji State Modernization Efforts in Kitahara Hakushū's *Memories*   19

2. Sexuality, Censorship, and State Critique in Hagiwara Sakutarō   44

3. "Fragrant Spaces Between Words": The Oblique Sexuality of Fragrance in Yonezawa Nobuko and Ōte Takuji   74

4. *Ice Land* and *Black Cypress*: Lyric Poetry and Photography in a Time of Total War   97

5. Oral Culture and the Poetry of Officially Licensed State Critique   113

Conclusion: "Poetry Gods" and the Legacy of Officially Licensed Poetry   131

Acknowledgments   135

Notes   137

Bibliography   151

…
LYRIC POETRY AS STATE CRITICISM IN MODERN JAPAN

Introduction
The Politics of Lyric and the Poetry of Officially Licensed State Critique

"Why Is This Self of Mine So Sad?": The Pan Society and Lyric Utopian Longing

In April 1909, a poetry and visual arts group called the Pan Society (Pan no Kai) discovered that two Japanese police officers had attended at least one of their meetings. According to the poet Kinoshita Mokutarō's (木下杢太郎, 1885–1945) recollections in 1926, it was rumored that the two policemen made a halfhearted attempt at surveillance, drinking sake in a Japanese-style room next door while the poets and artists met at a European-style restaurant called Eitai Tei in the Fukagawa neighborhood of Tokyo.[1] The Pan Society was a decadent organization, dedicated to drinking, poetry, and song, whose meetings took place at Western-style restaurants along the Sumida River, modeling itself on Parisian cafe culture along the River Seine. So instrumental was the Pan Society to the start of cafe culture in Tokyo that the group is often mentioned in histories of coffeeshops in Japan.[2] Café Printemps, which opened in the Ginza neighborhood in 1911 and is sometimes referred to as the first café in Tokyo, would later serve as one of their meeting places, but in 1909, before there were many cafes open in Tokyo, the Pan Society members had to content themselves with restaurants like Eitai Tei. The organization was not only concerned with Western culture, however. It also sought to replicate the atmosphere of the Edo period (1603–1867), as depicted in ukiyo-e prints and other popular art forms. Kinoshita states, "The Pan Society was the product of longing for the Edo atmosphere, for the atmosphere of foreign countries."[3] Kinoshita's language is lyrical and expressive: He suggests that the Pan Society was a product of "longing" (憧憬, *shōkei*) for a certain "atmosphere" (情調, *jōchō*). It is a poetics of longing and emotion that the Pan Society members espouse, one that partakes of the elements of lyric poetry, the expression of personal feelings in poetic form.

Why were the police concerned with this organization, whose biggest real-world concern seemed to be finding a good place to drink until late into the night? It is notable that the police chose a Japanese-style room for their vigil, in contrast to the would-be café, where the poets expressed their yearning for the West and for Edo. As Pan Society poet Yoshii Isamu (吉井勇, 1886–1960) explained it, the police misunderstood the name of the organization. Lacking familiarity with Western classics, they had not understood that the Pan Society was named after Pan, the Greek god of song. Instead, they assumed the poetry circle had named itself after the Japanese word for "bread," a Portuguese loan word also pronounced *pan*, and suspected the group of communist or proletarian sympathies due to the associations between bread and socialism found in works such as the anarchist Kōtoku Shūsui's (幸徳秋水, 1871–1911) 1909 translation of Peter Kropotkin's *The Conquest of Bread* (1892).[4][5] Even if the police were wrong about the meaning of the word pan, Pan Society poets did in fact embed their work with obliquely subversive aspects, making them of interest to the state for more than their writings about and real-life practice of decadence and pleasure.

Perhaps the "longing" Kinoshita describes was utopic in nature, though of course, it also had to do with the very real and urgent concern of finding a good place to drink and discuss poetry. According to Yoshii, the poets of Pan Society had a drinking song, a piece by the poet Kitahara Hakushū (北原白秋, 1885–1942), a member of the group, that they liked to sing together:

Bright Red Cloud in the Sky
Bright red cloud in the sky.
Bright red wine in the glass.
Why is this self of mine so sad?
Bright red cloud in the sky.

空に真赤（まっか）な
空（そら）に真赤（まっか）な雲（くも）のいろ。
玻璃（はり）に真赤（まっか）な酒（さけ）の色。
なんでこの身（み）が悲（かな）しかろ。
空（そら）に真赤（まっか）な雲（くも）のいろ。[6]

The poem was written in May 1908 and published in March of 1909 in Kitahara's debut poetry collection *Heretics*, which was noted for its use of red both in its poems and its lavish book design. The color red's associations with socialism go back at least to the Paris Commune of 1871, but it was also the signature color of *Heretics*. It is possible that the color red produced yet another misunderstanding that led the police to flag the group.

While the poem is not an ode to socialism, it does give voice to a certain utopic longing in a world transformed by modernity. The poem's songlike form recalls both Western free verse and Edo-period popular songs, and its 7–5 syllabic rhythm hearkens back even further to the long tradition of premodern *waka* poetry. Discussing this poem, Nakamura Shin'ichirō invokes both the modernists of Paris (who the Pan Society poets anticipate by about a decade) and the court poets of the thirteenth-century imperial anthology *Shin-kokinshū* (新古今集).[7] The poem expresses yearning for a time and place when poetry had a recognized social function—whether the cafes of nineteenth-century Europe (evoked by the glass, which was introduced to Japan following contact with the West), the court banquets of premodern Japan, or some unimagined future time. In the absence of any sense of connection or social belonging, the speaker feels alienated for reasons he is unable to articulate, an elusive sense of sadness. It is this sadness that, as Theodor Adorno says, "flashes out abruptly" and gives the reader a sense of the poem's historical moment.[8] Adorno, writing in 1957, many years after the Pan Society stopped meeting in 1913, defines lyric poetry as a utopic enterprise, as "the subjective expression of a social antagonism" that gives voice to the fragmentation of the self in industrial society.[9] Perhaps, on some level, it was the Pan Society's intense yearning for the world to be otherwise that attracted police attention.

This book seeks to understand the complex situation between the state and lyric poetry in the first half of the twentieth century in Japan. I use the term "officially licensed" poetry, inspired by a passage by the poet Hagiwara Sakutarō (萩原朔太郎, 1886–1942), to describe this delicate negotiation, one that hovers between resistance and complicity with the state. After all, during their vigil at the nearby drinking establishment, the police left the Pan Society alone, creating a sense of tacit permission. The Pan Society poets and artists were free to sing their potentially subversive songs of utopian longing, so long as they remained within the scope of what was permissible by the state. Lyric's subversive potential lies in its utopian longing for a different world, its ability to say while unsaying.

More specifically, this book locates prewar Japanese lyric poets' critical agency in their ability to navigate the fraught space between resistance and complicity in Japanese society in the first half of the twentieth century. The title's phrase "'Officially Licensed' State Critique" comes from an obscenity case discussed further in chapter 2, in which Hagiwara situates his work as collaborative with the same censorship regime he critiques. This book investigates Hagiwara's thoughtful, ambivalent self-positioning as a collaborator with the state who is nevertheless critical of its practices. When he in 1917 adopted the pose of an "officially licensed" poet, he insightfully described the position of lyric poetry in twentieth-century Japan, inextricably caught up in the very invisible structures it sought to make legible and thence to transform.

Lyric Poetry: The Personal and the Political

The Japanese word for lyric, a Chinese loan word pronounced *jojō* (抒情), means "to express emotion." The first character, meaning to convey or express, is related to the characters for the controller of a water container or the weaving device of a loom. It suggests that the act of conveying a feeling is similar to either containing a liquid or weaving a textile. The second character, meaning feeling or emotion, "as a core concept of the Chinese poetics of *qing* (情, feeling), has always indicated an interaction between the self and the world and beyond," according to David Der-Wei Wang.[10] Lyric in Japan operates as a bridge between self and world, influenced by the Chinese tradition, as well as by the West, in which the poetics of personal emotion are inextricably connected with social and political concerns. The bridge between self and world that is lyric poetry sometimes allows for political critique, but it also allows for collaboration and complicity with the state apparatus in Japan, sometimes both within the course of the same poem.

Let us look at a series of poetic images in which self and world intertwine. One night, a little boy wakes up in the room he shares with his brother to nightmares that draw on warrior tales from the local cinema to express fears of the cholera epidemics that affected the turn-of-the-century Japanese countryside. A detective follows a suspect through the city streets, afraid that he might be the very criminal he pursues. A brotherhood of thieves vows eternal loyalty in the dark of night. A lone nude woman applies perfume to her own body. A photograph in a magazine depicts a soldier, his eyes hidden from the viewer by bandages, and the magazine reader is so overcome that he has to look away.

These images, all drawn from poems studied in this book, point to a lyrical history of the years 1911 to 1940 in Japan, a snapshot of what they looked and felt like. One truth that emerges from these images is that there is no such thing as unmediated feeling during this period, when mass media was so highly present in everyday life. Each powerful emotion described is filtered through the lens of the mass media, whether it is cinema, the tropes of crime fiction, the commercial scent industry, or magazine photography. Part of what it meant to express emotion in this period was to engage the mass media, where people's deepest fears and desires resided. Lyric poetry's utopian longing for the world to be different entails a realignment between poetry, so often perceived as a high art form removed from the realm of popular culture, and the mass media, during this period an emerging phenomenon. As we shall see, Hagiwara's "On the Day of the Fall of Nanking" appeared in a mass media newspaper. What does it mean to voice a moment of impossible lyric longing for another world in the pages of a national newspaper, where Benedict Anderson has argued that the "imagined community" of the nation state takes form? In his ambivalent poem of resistance and complicity with the state war effort, Hagiwara gives voice to the cracks and fissures at work in the imagined community of the nation state in 1930s Japan. Mass media is important because it is a place where lyric poetry can hide in plain sight, obliquely expressing its subversive yearning for a different world.

Case Study: "On the Day of the Fall of Nanking"

For example, Hagiwara's only patriotic war poem was printed in a mass media newspaper, a salient example of officially licensed state critique. Hagiwara was ambivalent about his patriotic piece: A 1937 letter from Hagiwara to his colleague, the poet Maruyama Kaoru (丸山薫, 1899-1974) claims that he wrote a poem titled

"On the Day of the Fall of Nanking" in a single night after being "coercively requested" (強制的にたのまれ, *kyōsei-teki ni tanomare*) by a columnist for the *Tokyo Asahi Shinbun* newspaper.[11] Fear ran rampant in Japanese literary circles after proletarian writer Kobayashi Takiji (小林多喜二, 1903–33) was tortured to death by the police, suggesting that the coercive nature of the request to write the poem might have been quite real and intense. In the letter to Maruyama, Hagiwara went on to say that he "felt as if I joined the ranks of Saijō Yaso, and I can hardly stand the shame."[12] Saijō Yaso (西条八十, 1892–1970) was a commercially successful songwriter, children's writer, and poet. Saijō produced numerous patriotic works during the wartime period. To be included in the ranks of these national poets was, for Hagiwara, a source of shame. Nevertheless, he joins them, willingly or not.

The poem in question, "On the Day of the Fall of Nanking" (南京陥落の日に, "Nankin kanraku no hi ni," 1937), was published in the *Asahi Shinbun* to celebrate the Japanese conquest of Nanjing in 1937, an atrocity often referred to as the Rape of Nanjing or the Nanjing Massacre, in which the Japanese military killed over 300,000 civilians, according to many estimates. The poem is undoubtedly nationalistic in its sympathetic portrayal of Japanese soldiers and especially in its total silence concerning their victims; however it also expresses ambivalence towards the misery of warfare, and describes it in far from glamorous terms. The poem's critical valences toward warfare are often overlooked, and it is frequently omitted from anthologies of Hagiwara's work. It is widely considered a work of collaboration by literary critics and ordinary readers alike.[13] Recent scholars like Tsuboi Hideto have sought to complicate this view of the understudied poem.[14]

On the Day of the Fall of Nanking
The year is just about to end,
and soldiers' bayonets glare white.
Their war record has passed through summer and fall,
and past Shanghai this evening has already covered 100,000 kilometers.
Our troops marching without rest,

men and horses race one another onwards,
the Transportation Corps continues on the road of mud.
Ah, those who fight in this vast plain
all swear not to hope to return alive,

wearing iron helmets, burned by the sun.
The air is cold, the sun is freezing.
The year is just about to end.
Here Nanking will fall.
Raise our flag of the rising sun.
Now everyone's worries are about to be relieved,
and our victory is decided.
We must celebrate and cheer, banzai!
We must cry out and cheer, banzai!

南京陥落の日に
歳まさに暮れんとして
兵士の銃剣は白く光れり。
軍旅の暦は夏秋をすぎ
ゆうべ上海を抜いて百千キロ。
わが行軍の日は憩はず
人馬先に爭ひ走りて
輜重は泥濘の道に續けり。
ああこの曠野に戰ふもの
ちかつて皆生歸を期せず
鐵兜きて日に燒けたり。

天寒く日は凍り
歳まさに暮れんとして
南京ここに陥落す。
あげよ我等の日章旗
人みな愁眉をひらくの時
わが戰勝を決定して
よろしく萬歳を祝ふべし。
よろしく萬歳を叫ぶべし。[15]

Hagiwara's poem describes a scene of Japanese soldiers in transit, emphasizing their experiences of hardship. While their hard work and determination are portrayed in laudatory terms ("marching without rest," 行軍の日は憩わず, *kōgun no hi wa ikowazu*), they also appear dehumanized and animal-like, covered in mud and marching in formation with nonhuman horses. They appear to have given up their humanity for a life of subhuman, muddy labor and misery. The soldiers are not particularly warrior-like or brave; they participate in no scenes of combat, instead playing the role of beasts of burden hauling their load. The pitiful misery of the soldiers obscures their participation in the massacre; it is hard to imagine these figures of drudgery committing acts of extreme violence against Chinese civilians, who are not alluded to at all. The poem's attention to the sufferings of the soldiers thus serves to camouflage the brutality of the event it commemorates.

The smokescreen of the soldiers' suffering also has another function: it allows the poem to implicate its readers as fellow laborers in the wartime work force. The poem's description of the soldiers as grimy, dull working men, "wearing iron helmets, burned by the sun" (鐵兜きて日に燒けたり, *tetsu kabuto kite hi ni yaketari*), has a normalizing effect, rendering the extreme event in mundane, unexciting terms reminiscent of a long, hard commute to a factory or a construction site. By viewing the Nanjing Massacre through the lens of the Transportation Corps, Hagiwara highlights its connection to ordinary civilian life, its roots in the everyday routine of capitalistic labor. It is not only the Transportation Corps who experience a grueling work routine, after all; it is also the civilian labor force back in Tokyo who manufacture the goods the soldiers haul to the battlefield.

Further muddying the waters, the poem ends with a jingoistic cheer: "We must celebrate and cheer banzai! / We must celebrate and cheer banzai!" But there are overtones of coercion to the cheer that undermine its sincerity ("must celebrate," 祝ふべし, *iwau beshi*), so that the poem ends on a note of jingoism fraught with ambivalence. Perhaps Hagiwara's disavowal of the poem, his claim to have dashed it off under duress, forms part of the provocation posed by the final lines' forced cry of banzai: The border between coerced participation in the war effort and genuine enthusiasm becomes illegible, leaving its audience of newspaper readers with plenty to puzzle over regarding their own participation in the mass media home front.

When read in its original setting in the pages of the *Asahi Shimbun*, it is striking how the poem's line breaks create a sense of aporia or rupture in the visual form of the newspaper page.[16] In a dense block of text and images, the white space of the poem offers the reader a pause of empty space to reflect and speculate. Are readers, like the tired soldiers of the poem, slogging mechanically through their routine of participation in the war effort as mass media consumers; or do they experience moments of jingoistic pleasure in their work? What are the thoughts and intentions behind Hagiwara's new self-positioning as a reluctant national poet? It is interesting to think of this poem in dialogue with Hagiwara's description of his work as "officially licensed poetry" in 1917, at the beginning of his career. Twenty years later, "On the Day of the Fall of Nanking" could also be a kind of "officially licensed poetry," offering oblique criticism of the very same state institutions that it is enlisted to support.

1911–40: A Historical Period of Officially Licensed State Critique in Japan

The study of Japanese poetry through this lens of officially licensed state critique requires the explanation of three points: the historical background of the period, the mass media's essential role, and the methodology of close reading. The years 1911 to 1940 involved popular mobilization accompanied by brutal state repression. These years in Japan span time from three emperors' reigns: the Meiji period (1868-1912), the Taishō period (1912-26), and the Shōwa period (1926-89). This fraught era saw the end of late-Meiji-period socialist and labor activism in the wake of the executions related to the Great Treason Incident in 1910 to 1911 and the establishment of the Special Higher Police in 1911, with the power to investigate political crimes and dissent. Another round of brutal police repression of labor movements followed in the aftermath of the 1923 Great Kantō Earthquake and the 1925 Peace Preservation Law. These years also witnessed Japan's emergence on the world stage as an imperial power in Asia competing with Western nations, as well as the rise of militarism and imperialism in the 1930s. The fifteen-year period from 1930 to 1945 is sometimes referred to as a "dark valley" by historians of Japan, a time when Taishō Japan's earlier democratic promise and potential failed to realize, and the Japanese empire committed horrific atrocities in the areas of Asia over which it ruled.[17] Twentieth-century Japanese lyric poets wrote during this time of transition, brutality, and turbulence, and it is in this charged atmosphere that they critiqued the Japanese state even as they were complicit in its endeavors. Steve Rabson's *Righteous Cause or Tragic Folly: Changing Views of War in Japanese Poetry* offers a survey of modern Japanese poetry about war, discussing antiwar poems, as well as patriotic prowar ones. Rabson shows how both registers, despite their differences, are implicated in their wartime contexts.

Also important is how these poets engaged with mass media, both as subject matter for their writing and as mode of disseminating their work. William Gardner's *Advertising Tower: Japanese Modernism and Modernity in the 1920s*, which describes how Japanese avant-garde poets of the 1920s engaged with mass culture, suggests that the mass media context is essential to understand modern Japanese poetry. The mass media emerged in Japan during the 1920s with the appearance of three nationally circulated newspapers, the beginning of radio broadcasting in 1925, and the widespread popularity of cinema in both the cities and countryside.[18] Drawing on photography, film, radio, records, and advertising, the four writers in this book operationalize lyric poetry itself as a mass medium, one capable of expressing the emotions of the collective. Mass media offered the poets of officially licensed state critique exposure to a wider audience, as well as the opportunity to hide in plain sight.

Studying the poetry of officially licensed state critique requires the methodology of close reading, the detailed formal and content-related analysis of literary works with particular attention to moments of ambiguity. Barbara Johnson once defined the skill of close reading as "[h]ow to notice things in a text that a speed-reading culture is trained to disregard, overcome, edit out, or explain away," suggesting that to close read a text is an ethical act in and of itself in today's information age.[19] My study, inspired by deconstructionists like Johnson, as well as the critics of the Frankfurt School, who also valued the attentive interpretation of literature, deepens the political and social significance of close reading by excavating the political valences of poetic texts, both critical and complicit. Close reading and political engagement can enrich each other in mutually rewarding ways, ways that are sometimes surprising or counterintuitive.

Endogenous Antecedents: Lyric and History

My study contributes to the ongoing debate in contemporary critical theory about the social relevance of lyric. Lyric has come in for valid criticism as hermetic, personal, and apolitical, and therefore irrelevant to cultural studies and critical theory, especially compared with narrative and fiction. However, thinkers such as Adorno and Walter Benjamin, and more recently Robert Kaufman and Christopher Nealon have argued specifically for the critical agency of lyric poetry.

Jonathan Stalling broadens this often Eurocentric debate about the politics of lyric to include a transpacific perspective, suggesting that Asian aesthetics and cultural notions influenced modern Western conceptions of poetry and politics. Stalling suggests that W. H. Auden's famous 1939 line "Poetry makes nothing happen" was inspired by Buddhistic concepts of nothingness and "anti-teleological indeterminacy," and that, politically, Auden's words represent "a move toward releasing the teleological ends of many core American values."[20] What does it mean to make nothing happen, and how does lyric poetry create possibilities for these acts of nothingness? The Asian influences upon many of the thinkers who explored the politicization of lyric lie beyond the scope of this study, but it is important to keep in mind that, for example, Adorno and Benjamin's work on lyric poetry would not have been possible without this transpacific flow of ideas. For example, Peter Fenves has written persuasively on Chinese influences in Benjamin's work, noting that a 1910 German translation by Richard Wilhelm of Laozi's *Daodejing* was among the books Benjamin took with him when he fled the Nazis as a refugee.[21] Christopher Bush argues that "a substantial relationship" to China exists in Benjamin's work, and that "[i]n sum, Benjamin's 'China' is tied up with his efforts to think the ways in which mimesis constitutes a second nature, specifically through the medium of human embodiment."[22] The political agency of lyric poetry is not a Western concept, and has roots in Asian poetics that synchronize with Western theorists.

Takayuki Tatsumi's work on the literary genre of cyberpunk proves instructive for the case of modern lyric poetry. Tatsumi argues that, rather than a linear model of Western influence and Eastern imitation, the cyberpunk genre represents "the indeterminate, unpredictable, and even chaotic dynamics between the orientalist gaze and the occidentalist one, without which we could not have constituted our own reality."[23] Tatsumi pushes us readers to consider the synchronicity and unevenness with which literary transactions between East and West take place, and not to hierarchically situate the West as an original to be imitated by the East. Similarly, Miryam Sas's *Fault Lines: Cultural Memory and Japanese Surrealism*, which traces the mechanisms of cultural memory that twentieth-century Japanese surrealists used to indigenize the European poetic movements they wrote in dialogue with, shows how binary understandings of imitation and original are wholly inadequate. Without East Asian understandings of lyric poetry as an inherently political form of expression, the theoretical frameworks employed by Benjamin, Adorno, and others mentioned here would not be possible.

In order to properly situate the poets discussed here, I will briefly sketch the intersection of lyric poetry and politics in Japan prior to the period 1911 to 1940. These historical periods have been extensively studied, and I will offer a few salient moments to consider the dynamic between politics and poetry, rather than a comprehensive literary history. The modern Japanese poets in this study draw on a long tradition of politically engaged poetry that engages the social world through the lens of personal feelings. This tradition goes back at least to the famous Japanese preface to the first imperial poetry anthology, *Kokinshū* (古今集), composed in the early tenth century. Attributed to aristocratic court poet Ki no Tsurayuki (紀貫之, 872-945), this text is often perceived as the foundation of Japanese poetics, and its influence extends to the modern day. The Japanese preface (there is also a preface in Chinese, which was used widely for literary composition among elite circles in this period in Japan) clearly establishes Japanese poetry as a mode of personal feeling embedded in the social world:

> The seeds of Japanese poetry lie in the human heart and grow into leaves of ten thousand words. Many things happen to the people of this world, and all that they think and feel is given expression in description of things they see and hear. When we hear the warbling of the mountain thrush in the blossoms or the voice of the frog in the water, we know every living being has its song.
>
> It is poetry which, without effort, moves heaven and earth, stirs the feelings of the invisible gods and spirits, smooths the relations of men and women, and calms the hearts of fierce warriors.

> やまとうたは、人のこころをたねとして、よろづのことのはとぞなれりける、世中にある人、ことわざしげきものなれば、心におもふことを見るものきくものにつけていひいだせるなり、花になくうぐひす、水にすむかはづのこゑをきけば、いきとしいけるものいづれかうたをよまざりける、ちからをもいれずしてあめつちをうごかし、めに見えぬおに神をもあはれとおもはせ、をとこをむなのなかをもやはらげ、たけきもののふの心をもなぐさむるは、うたなり[24]

The *Kokinshū* preface describes Japanese poetry (specifically, the classical thirty-one syllable genre of *waka*) as a mode for the expression of personal feelings. At the same time, it also highlights the social functions of *waka* poetry, such as politically fraught courtship between men and women (which, while deeply personal, could also determine the fate of political dynasties), or calming "the hearts of fierce warriors" (たけきもののふの心をもなぐさむる, *takeki mono no fu no kokoro o mo nagusamuru*). The two functions, personal and social, intertwine inextricably in the mode of *waka* poetry.

In addition to the *Kokinshū* preface, it is instructive to look at another moment from premodern Japanese poetics, the waka poet Fujiwara Teika's (藤原定家, 1162–1241) famous "crimson banners remark," a passage from his Chinese-language diary called *Meigetsuki* (明月記). Teika was a political court figure in addition to being an accomplished poet. His rocky relationship with the retired Emperor Go-Toba (後鳥羽, 1180–1239) led to the compilation of the influential imperial poetry anthology, the thirteenth-century *Shin-kokinshū*. In a diary entry dated to the ninth month of 1180, Teika notes the ongoing war between two clans, the Minamoto and the Taira, in the following terms:

> [Reports of] sedition and punitive forces in the realm fill my ears, but I shall not record them. Crimson banners and the conquest of barbarians are no business of mine.[25]

Paul S. Atkins explains that "the 'crimson banners' refers to the Taira family's war colors and 'the conquest of barbarians' refers to a punitive expedition sent against the Minamoto by the court at the behest of the Taira patriarch, Kiyomori."[26] This passage presents the poet as removed from worldly affairs, including warfare and court intrigue between powerful factions, when in fact Teika was deeply implicated in politics. As Ivo Smits argues, "no matter how often he might vow that 'crimson banners' had nothing to do with his art, the political situations in which he found himself dictated otherwise."[27] Teika's provocative note, which reveals his precedents in classical Chinese poetics by rewriting a line from Tang poet Bai Juyi (白居易, 772–846), poses the question: What are the politics of removing oneself from the world of the "crimson banners," the social and political realm? How is this pose of removal from politics itself a kind of political intervention?

The social and political significance of poetry in Japan continued into the modern period, with which this study is concerned. An anthology of mostly Anglo-American poetry translations called *Shintaishi* (new-style poetry) *Selections* (新体詩抄, *Shintaishi-shō*) appeared in 1882, edited by German philosophy major Inoue Tetsujirō (井上哲次郎, 1855–1944), sociologist Toyama Masakazu (外山正一, 1848–1900), and botanist Yatabe Ryōkichi (矢田部良吉, 1851–99). It is notable that none of the *Shintaishi Selections* editors were primarily poets. The fact that a philosopher, a botanist, and a sociologist would concern themselves with these questions already shows something about poetry's relevance to the social world at this time. Scott Mehl discusses how the *shintaishi* poets' formal innovation

> was intertwined with parallel conversations about Japan's putative standing on an international stage. Ideological concerns were at the forefront of critics' minds: as Japanese writers and thinkers weighed the meaning of Japan's new entanglements with the governments and cultures of Europe and North America, they found it necessary to rethink what it meant to write poetry in Japanese.[28]

The *shintaishi* poets thus combined formal innovation with ideological awareness of the social world. Inoue included the following comments in his preface to a translation of a poem by American poet Henry Wadsworth Longfellow (1807–82), whose work portrayed his personal feelings and autobiographical themes for a mass audience:

> The waka [歌, uta] of Meiji should be the waka of Meiji, not the waka of the past. Japanese poetry written in classical Chinese [詩, shi] should be Japanese poetry, not Chinese poetry [漢詩, kanshi]. This is the reason for composing poetry in the new style [新體ノ詩, shintai no shi].
>
> 明治ノ歌ハ、明治ノ歌ナルベシ、古歌ナルベカラズ、日本ノ詩ハ日本ノ詩 ナルベシ、漢詩ナルベカラズ、是レ新體ノ詩ノ作ル所似ナリ[29]

This passage reveals how the inventors of the new term *shintaishi*, or new-style poetry, were wrestling with the different genres of Japanese poetry, including thirty-one-syllable *waka* and poetry written in classical Chinese, in order to create something they perceived as new. In creating this new poetic genre, Inoue also makes a powerful argument for the social value of poetry, indicating that Meiji Japan needed a form of expression capable of describing its specific social and political conditions. When Inoue comments that "the *waka* of Meiji should be the waka of Meiji" (明治ノ歌ハ、明治ノ歌ナルベシ, *Meiji no uta wa, Meiji no uta naru beshi*), he highlights the social relevance of his work, and of poetry more generally. The statement has a tautological quality, so that Meiji *waka* is so unique and singular that it can only be described by itself.

The late Meiji period saw politically inflected works by poets Kitamura Tōkoku (北村透谷, 1868–94) and his friend and disciple Shimazaki Tōson (島崎藤村, 1872–1943). Maeda Ai has described Kitamura's

1889 extended poem "A Prisoner's Song" (楚囚之詩, *Soshū no shi*) as a meditation on "the trauma experienced by Tōkoku for having left the Freedom and Popular Rights Movement," a Meiji-period political movement for liberal democracy in Japan.[30] As for Tōson, whose *Collection of Young Greens* (若菜集, *Wakanashū*) was one of the defining works of the new genre of *shintaishi* in 1897, Michael Bourdaghs has written that his "highly personal and emotional poetry has, from early on, been linked with the politics of Meiji nationalism."[31] For both poets, lyric poetry was inextricably linked with politics. Robert Tuck's *Idly Scribbling Rhymers: Poetry, Print, and Community in Nineteenth-Century Japan* describes how Meiji period poets like Masaoka Shiki (正岡子規, 1867-1902) cultivated poetry's relationship to the "imagined community" of the Meiji Japanese nation-state.

By contrast, lyric poetry by late Meiji writers like Tayama Katai (田山花袋, 1871-1930), Yanagita Kunio (柳田國男, 1875-1965), Miyazaki Koshoshi (宮崎湖処子, 1864-1922), and Kunikida Doppo (国木田独歩, 1871-1908) featured an often hermetic sense of a closed, personal realm at once removed from the social world and embedded within it. In an essay by Yanagita included in the 1897 volume *Lyric Poetry* (抒情詩, *Jojōshi*), the famous poet, critic, and founder of ethnography in Japan displays a sense of lyric poetry as a personally expressive enterprise as "our very own song" separate from "the law of the world":

> In our opinion, the future success of this thing we call free verse ["*shintaishi*"] depends on forgetting the self in words and rhythm, on many people allowing almost any of the various means relied upon by our hearts, to utterly and boldly express or thoughts as they are. Thus, these shall be our very own songs, and indeed this form and this use of language, though there is much to mark their difference from the law of the world, are all the more our own, expressing our thought and feeling [我が思を舒べたる, *waga omoi o nobetaru*], our very own song.
>
> 思ふに、此新體詩といふもの々、行末さかえなむ爲には、我を忘れて、言葉に、調に、さまゞと心を盡したまふ人も多きに、膽太くもかく思のまゝなる事を言ひ出でむは、殆許さるまじきわざなるべし、されどいかにせん、此は我が歌なり、よし此姿此言葉づかひ、世のさだめに違ふこと多くとも、猶これはわが思を舒べたる、我が歌なるをや。[32]

Yanagita notably uses the character 舒 to mean "expressing" (舒べたる, *nobetaru*), which David Der-Wei Wang says is related etymologically to the character 抒 (*jo*) in 抒情 (*jojō*), or lyric.³³ This verb directly connects Yanagita's poetics of feeling to the word for lyric: It is lyric poetry that will serve as the expressive vehicle which Yanagita imagines. James R. Morita argues that "[t]he key note of the *Jojōshi* poets may be summed up as 'nostalgia,' while that of the *Shintaishi* poets was *bunmei kaika*, or 'enlightenment.'"³⁴ While the *shintaishi* poets gave voice to the Meiji period's own unique song, the *Lyric Poetry* poets fifteen years later sought a poetics of pure feeling and expression, to give voice to their own personal song. The optimistic, almost naive political outlook of the *shintaishi* poets has given way to the self-conscious ambivalence towards the political world adopted by the *jojōshi* poets.

Yanagita's comment that poets rely on "forgetting the self" (我を忘れて, *ware o wasurete*) is particularly interesting: In the act of expressing his own personal feelings, the poet gives voice to the oblivion of the self. This phrase about forgetting the self recalls, or rather anticipates, the lineage of critical theory that sees in lyric a utopian utterance of the extinguishment of the modern capitalistic notion of selfhood. Even in an essay devoted to a poetics of pure personal feeling, the cracks and fissures of the lyric form show themselves, and through these cracks, politics and history emerge.

Conclusion and Chapter Breakdown

The poets treated in this study each negotiate the complex position of "officially licensed" state critique in a different way, using lyric poetry as an institutionally permissible mode of dissent. Chapter 1's lyric poet Kitahara uses poetic recollections of his childhood to lay out a multi-pronged critique of the Meiji state's efforts at modernization, addressing the state's involvement in institutionalized health efforts, the implication of photography in the construction of imperial power, and the top-down imposition of modern industrial clock time. Kitahara's work provides the foundation for the argument in the following chapters by showing how lyric poetry does not take a direct political stance, but rather, expresses its state critique in the language of emotional and sensory private experience. It is through the eyes of a child that Kitahara makes legible the dark side of history and poetically illuminates that which is left behind by the Meiji ideology of teleological progress.

In chapter 2, Hagiwara positions himself as what he calls an "officially licensed" poet during his 1917 obscenity case, and he collaborates with the censors to make his critiques of Japanese society legible in the pages of his small poetry magazine *Sentiment* (感情, *Kanjō*). Like Kitahara, Hagiwara adopts a position of "officially licensed" state critique, so that his critique of state efforts to regulate obscenity and sexual morals does not speak the language of public life and politics. Rather, Hagiwara's critique remains in the register of the personal inner life of the poet, using his powerfully psychological poetry to make a political critique of compulsory heterosexuality and state efforts to regulate nonnormative sexual practices, including homosexuality, cross-dressing, and non-reproductive sex.

In chapter 3, poets Yonezawa Nobuko (米澤順子, 1894–1931) and Ōte Takuji (大手拓次, 1887–1934) build on Hagiwara's critique of state efforts to regulate sexuality and morals. Yonezawa and Ōte use imagery of fragrance and smell to obliquely argue for a world where androgyny, same-sex desire, and sexual fluidity are lauded as the basis of poetic creation, not marginalized as backward and uncivilized in favor of modern heterosexuality. Because of state efforts to promote compulsory heterosexuality to appeal to a Western gaze and position Japan as a modern nation-state, Yonezawa and Ōte's portrayal of nonnormative sexuality operates powerfully on the level of state critique.

In chapter 4, poetry collections by Kitahara and Hagiwara, written in the 1930s during the Pacific War, express ambivalence toward the war's overpowering presence in daily life. Kitahara was a prolific producer of nationalistic poetry, while Hagiwara only ever produced the one highly ambivalent war poem, "On the Day of the Fall of Nanking," as we have seen. The two poets thus came at the question of what it means to write poetry in a time of total war from two very different perspectives. Kitahara expresses his self-conscious awareness of complicity in the national war effort, while Hagiwara writes from a more ambivalent, critical position. What the two poets have in common is that they operate in the realm of the personal, while addressing the political. Of course, the strictures of militarism and censorship make direct political critique all but impossible at this historical moment in time. Rather, by confining their melancholy, lamenting poems to the tedium, ennui, and painfulness of everyday life, the two poets work together to show the suffocating effects of war on the supposedly separate realm of the civilian quotidian.

Chapter 5 describes how ambivalent vocal performances by Hagiwara and Kitahara show the poets' critical attitude toward the militarization of daily life, especially its encroachment into the realm of cinema and media. In this chapter, the poets' political critique operates by approaching the carefully regulated realm of mass media from the perspective of lyric poetry. Their laments for a passing era of cinema as the transition to sound occurs echoes with ambivalence toward their own role as national poets tasked with producing propagandistic verse. In the realm of officially licensed poetry, they lament their own complicity in state efforts to nationalize poetry alongside other media forms.

Kitahara and Hagiwara are both major poets in Japan, while Yonezawa and Ōte are more minor. This book is not intended as a comprehensive account of modern Japanese poetry. Rather, these poets are case studies in how poets negotiate the complex situations of their historical period: sometimes with degrees of resistance, and sometimes with complicity. The poets of officially licensed state critique bring to light human beings' embeddedness in structures just beyond their comprehension, and the brief moments when those structures flash into partially sensed legibility. They act as models of oblique political engagement. Together, these poets indicate a mode of lyricism as a mass idiom, one which proposes, not only the solitary concerns of an individual poet, but a politically engaged imaginary for the collective. At the very least, the lyric poet acts as a model of oblique political engagement for the crowd, occupying a privileged place with whom the collective can identify. What are the poetic and political possibilities of receding from the worldly realm? These are the ethical and aesthetic questions that ground this study.

CHAPTER 1

Critiquing Meiji State Modernization Efforts in Kitahara Hakushū's *Memories*

Pan Society founder and experimental poet Kitahara Hakushū, like other Pan Society members, employed the genre of lyric poetry to imaginatively engage with his political moment. In Kitahara's 1911 poetry collection *Memories: Small Lyric Songs* (思ひ出：抒情小曲集, *Omoide: Jojō shōkyoku-shū*), the poet's childhood memories become a vehicle for a critique of the Meiji state, which, at the time, was rapidly modernizing Japan along the lines of a nineteenth-century nation-state. Kitahara captures the effects of these modernization efforts on the everyday sensations and experiences of a small child in Yanagawa, Kyushu.

Kitahara is a major, canonical Japanese poet who worked in free verse, *tanka* (a classical poetry form in thirty-one syllables, often used to mean the same as *waka*), folk songs, and children's poetry. *Memories* was one of the works that launched his career. *Memories* was Kitahara's second free verse collection, the follow-up to his debut book *Heretics* (邪宗門, *Jashūmon*) in 1909, from which came the Pan Society's drinking song discussed above. *Heretics* was influenced by *Sounds of the Tide* (海潮音, *Kaichō'on*, 1905), a book of translations by Ueda Bin (上田敏, 1874–1916), which included poets like Paul Verlaine (1844–1896) and Emile Verhaeren (1855–1916). Kitahara was also influenced by translations by Mori Ōgai (森鴎外, 1862–1922), such as his rendering of Hans

Christian Andersen's *The Improvisatore* from 1902.¹ The collection *Heretics* features intense fascination with early modern encounters in Japan with Portugal and Holland, an aesthetic often known as *nanban*, or "southern barbarians." The *nanban* style of visual art and material culture was popular in the late Meiji period, and Kitahara was caught up in this vogue for early modern encounters with the West.² In summer of 1907, Kitahara went on a trip with other members of the Pan Society to his hometown Yanagawa, Amagusa, Nagasaki, and Shimabara, sites associated with these early modern Western encounters and the *nanban* aesthetic. He and his cotravelers, who included *tanka* poets Yosano Tekkan (与謝野鉄幹, 1873–1935) and Hirano Banri (平野万里, 1885–1947), as well as Kinoshita Mokutarō and Yoshii Isamu, would produce a collection of travel writings based on their journey, *Five Pairs of Shoes* (五足の靴, *Go-soku no kutsu*, 1907).

Written largely in syllabic units of fives and sevens, *Heretics* combines this fascination with the exotic West with a youthful, rebellious spirit. One of its most famous poems, "Rebellion" (*Muhon*, 謀叛) is often read as a declaration toward Kitahara's mentor Yosano, whose coterie journal *Morning Star* (明星, *Myōjō*, 1900–1908) Kitahara would leave in 1908.³ Another feature of *Heretics* is its rich, often very difficult vocabulary, which combines Western imports, classical Japanese, and poetic neologisms. Kinoshita once notably compared the collection to "a broken kaleidoscope" in which disparate time periods, cultures, and emotions were chaotically refracted.⁴ Fukasawa states that *Heretics* "signaled the beginning of a new era in Japanese symbolist poetry as well as an important milestone in the development of truly modern verse in Japanese."⁵

Memories represents a continuation of the bold experimentation found in *Heretics*. Many of the poems in *Memories* first appeared in small poetry journals, such as *Pleiades* (スバル, *Subaru*, 1909–13), which was affiliated with the Pan Society, or Yosano's *Morning Star* before Kitahara and Yosano's rift. Following the publication of *Memories*, Kitahara published a *tanka* collection called *Paulownia Flowers* (桐の花, *Kiri no hana*, 1913). This collection was in part inspired by his turn to Buddhism following the trauma of a two-week imprisonment for an adulterous affair with a woman who later became his first wife, Fukushima Toshiko (福島敏子; her married name when she met Kitahara was Matsushita, 松下). Due to economic necessity stemming from the failure of his parents' sake brewing business, Kitahara turned to writing children's poetry and folk songs in the 1920s and 1930s, meeting with commercial success. His work in *Memories*, which portrayed childhood and children, prefigures this turn to children's writing. He also produced a number of patriotic poems during the later years of his career, which will be discussed further in chapter 4.

Memories contains a lengthy autobiographical prose preface of ten numbered sections, followed by a short preface poem. The work is then made up of seven sections: "Queen of Hearts" (骨牌の女王, "Karuta no jo'ō"), "Fragments," (断章, "Danshō"), "Days Past" (過ぎし日, "Sugishi hi"), "Memories," (おもひで, "Omoide"), "Buds of Life" (生の芽生, "Sei no gasei"), "Tonka John's Sorrow" (TONKA JOHNの悲哀, "Tonka John no hiai"), and "Folk Songs of Yanagawa" (柳河風俗詩, "Yanagawa fūzoku uta"). There is also a series of illustrations, mostly drawings by Kitahara himself.

Each poem in *Memories* participates in the unveiling of contradictions and fissures at the heart of Japanese modernity as propagated by the Meiji state. Kitahara's poems provide a dimension of commentary on their social and political situation in their moments of rupture, in which the text undoes its own capacity to signify. These moments of rupture manifest as flashes of memory, wherein the past suddenly resurfaces into the present.

An "Inner Emigration" and the Reaction Against Late Meiji Lyric Poets

Kitahara was one of many poets following the late Meiji generation who sought to open lyric up to its social and political context without abandoning the personal, inward realm, operating in the realm of officially licensed state critique. *Memories*, published in the last years of the Meiji period, though many of its poems first appeared in magazines several years previously, was a turning point between the earlier form of *shintaishi* (new style poetry) written in classical Japanese, and *jiyūshi* (自由詩, free verse), written in modern day colloquial Japanese (*kōgo*, 口語), which would become the dominant idiom of poetry written in Japanese in the Taishō period. The language of *Memories*, as we shall see in the hybrid, chaotic vocabulary appearing in poems such as "Sun" and "Night," mixes grammatical patterns from classical Japanese with modern and Westernized neologisms, regional words from the Kyushu dialect spoken in Yanagawa, and terms from modern scientific vocabulary. Kitahara's younger contemporary, Hagiwara Sakutarō, would publish *Howling at the Moon* (月に吠える, *Tsuki ni Hoeru*), the first work of colloquial *jiyūshi*, in 1917, six years after the publication of *Memories*, citing Kitahara's work, and *Memories* in particular, as an important source of inspiration in his creation of a new poetic language.[6]

Kitahara's politically aware poems in *Memories* came at a time of a growing focus on personal, private expression in Japanese literature and intellectual life, and lively debate about the political possibilities of such an inward turn. Harry Harootunian has described this introspective turn as an "inner emigration" that favored "unpolitical" matters of the self over collective political action.[7] Harootunian suggests that this disenchantment with political action stemmed from the onset of nationalism and imperialism in Japanese public life beginning at the end of the nineteenth century, especially the series of Peace Preservation Laws first passed in 1900 that regulated labor activism and freedom of speech.[8] Many disaffected Japanese intellectuals chose to take a critical stance in art or literary work rather than in political action and looked to "literature and art as a new mediation between individual and state."[9] Harootunian suggests that the unpolitical turn of many Japanese literary and intellectual figures had a kind of critical overtone: "[f]ailure to change the world led to criticism of it."[10] The widespread disillusionment among writers and artists intensified during the "winter period" (冬の時代, *fuyu no jidai*) that followed the 1911 Great Treason Trial and the government's ensuing crackdown on leftist speech and organizing.[11] The inner emigration brought with it a newly inward-facing mode of socially and politically engaged writing.

This sense of lyric as a form in crisis was intensified by the pervasive inward turn in Japanese intellectual life in response to increases in state surveillance and regulation of expression, such as the attempt to monitor the Pan Society. The cracks and fissures already apparent in lyric form for the turn-of-the-century poets of the "winter period" become an opportunity for Kitahara's experiments with officially licensed critique in *Memories*.

Yanagawa as Machine, Projection, and Nightmare in *Memories*

Kitahara's machine-like portrayal of Yanagawa suggests his "critical stance towards the government's policy of modernization" in modern spaces such as both Yanagawa and Tokyo, a stance that he unfolds over the course of the collection.[12] Kitahara once compared his rapid-fire, imagistic writing style to the speed of cinema: "The film that has been granted me is cut extremely short. My speed is fairly rapid: it is light, it is shadow, it is color, it is pure sound. Watch the film as it goes *cut cut cut* [*patsu patsu patsu*]."¹³ His evocations of Yanagawa are written in a mechanized style, saturated in the visual cultures of the late Meiji period, perhaps in part due to his having lived in Tokyo since 1904 when he moved there to pursue his literary career.

Kitahara's descriptions of his childhood home, the riverside city of Yanagawa on the southern island of Kyushu, use motifs drawn from Meiji-period cinema and other visual media to underline what he saw as the city's complicated relationship to the Meiji project of nation-building and modernization. Yanagawa was a former castle town with a network of canals built by its feudal landowning family during the Tokugawa period.¹⁴ The canal system was originally used for transportation and defense, but by the time Kitahara was born in 1885, it was widely perceived as a relic of an outdated time. The canals were at the center of concerns about modernity and hygiene. The Meiji state issued regulations in 1896 for the clean use of the canals, ordering residents not to dump waste.¹⁵ The canals were viewed as a relic of an earlier, pre-Meiji era that had to be regulated and controlled by modernity.

In *Memories*, the canals are represented as at once nostalgic figments of the past, and mechanistic objects of modernity. In the preface, the speaker describes the town's famous canals, often evoked in nostalgic terms as a connection to an Edo-period economy before train services and modern roads, as glowing with artificial light: "near and far, emitting silver light, many man-made waterways come into view" (遠く近く朧銀の光を放つてゐる幾多の人工的河水を眼にするであらう。).¹⁶ As has been said of Kitahara's portrayal of Tokyo, this description of Yanagawa's canals seems as if "he is not writing about a city at all but about a machine," a machine that, like a film projector or other Meiji-period mechanized visual entertainments, emits metallic light and directs the speaker's field of vision through space, "near and far."¹⁷ Kitahara's image constellation of hometown, canal system, and cinematic machine produces an ambivalent relationship to Meiji modernity, whereby Yanagawa is at once transformed into a mechanical entity by the process of modernization, as well as relegated to a vestigial, nostalgic status as a relic of the past.

Kitahara emphasizes the town's loss of economic prosperity. His family's once-thriving sake brewery had recently failed at the time of *Memories*'s publication, leaving Kitahara, already a successful poet thanks to *Heretics*, as the family's primary breadwinner. For Kitahara,

Yanagawa is a "dead city" (廢市, *haishi*), an "ash-colored coffin" (*hai-iro no hitsugi*, 灰色の柩), an inorganic machine that shines but does not produce anything but light.[18] Kitahara's coinage "dead city" would later resurface as the title of Fukunaga Takehiko's (福永武彦, 1918-79) 1959 novel, in which the narrator describes Yanagawa as a relic left behind by the forward progress of history: "What an old, yet beautiful town it was. There was a story that it had not once been bombed during the war, but why would the American planes burn this little, unproductive town left behind in history?" (何といふ古びた、しかし美しい街だったらう。戦争の間に一度も空襲を受けたことがないといふ話だつたが、こんな非生産的な歴史の中に取り残されてしまつたやうな小さな町を、アメリカの飛行機が焼く筈もなかつた。).[19] In this passage, Fukunaga draws on Kitahara's portrayal of Yanagawa to position it as a vestige left behind by the forward motion of historical progress, importantly describing the town as "unproductive" (非生産的な, *hiseisanteki na*), excluding it from capitalistic notions of utility and productiveness. Yanagawa, while affected by the mechanistic values of modernization, fails to keep up with the teleological progress of capitalistic time.

"Sun:" Cinema and the State in Kitahara's Childhood Memories

In the poem "Sun" (太陽, "*Taiyō*"), Kitahara reveals that his hometown is a constructed "projection of a town" mediated through emerging visual technologies that are policed and surveilled by the Meiji state. Like Kitahara's mechanized evocations of urban space in his writings on Tokyo as discussed by Evelyn Schulz, Yanagawa here appears as a figment in a "kaleidoscope" held by the speaker of the poem: It is a trick of perception like the play of light found in the device. The speaker then feels the surveilling presence of a judge at work in his inner self.

> **Sun**
> The sun is like a trumpet on a festival day,
> a magician's released doves,
> or a fluttering banner for a medicinal bath,
> or antipyrine powder from long ago.
> The sun, red then green,
> shines inside a kaleidoscope turning in a child's hands,
> smothered with grain blossoms,

penetrating the thin lens into the depth of my eerie box,
refracts again, like faint magic lantern dreams, projections
of a town.

The sun also sends pink silk trees to sleep,
blows and scatters gentle dandelion puffs.
For a silver harmonica, for the smell of autumn's harvest,
or for blue toads' skin, it eases an almost unbearable pain.

The sun comforts the glow of withered grass, the flavor of corn,
like a gentle older sister, and yet
the sun, the sun
on a new young man's awe—a secret that changes body and soul,
with the intensely glaring gaze of a judge,
ah, ah, the sun looks on and on, and watches menacingly.

太陽

太陽は祭日の喇叭のごとく、
放たれし手品つかひの鳩のごとく、
或は閃く薬湯のフラフのごとく、
なつかしきアンチピリンの粉のごとし。
太陽は紅く、また、みどりに、
幼年の手に回す万華鏡のなかに光り、
穀物の花にむせび、
薄きレンズを透かしてわが怪しき函のそこに、
微かなる幻燈のゆめのごとく、また街の射影をうつす。

太陽はまた合歓の木をねむらせ、
やさしきたんぽぽを吹きおくり、
銀のハーモニカに、秋の収穫のにほいに、
或は青き蟾蜍の肌に触れがたき痛みをちらす。
太陽は枯草のほめきに、玉蜀黍の風味に、
優しき姉のさまして労れども、
太陽は太陽は

新しき少年の恐怖(おそれ)にぞ——身と霊との変りゆく秘密にぞ、
あまりにも眩き判官(はんぐわん)のまなざしをもて
ああ、ああ、太陽はかにかくに凝視(みつ)めつつ脅かす。[20]

Influenced by symbolist poetry's use of synesthesia and sensory disorientation, the first stanza portrays the sun as a chaotic entity whose light manifests as sound (a trumpet), flight (the released doves), and intoxicating substance (the medicinal antipyrine), causing a feeling of synesthetic confusion in the speaker. Like the "silver light" emitted by the artificial waterways of Yanagawa in the preface, the light emitted by the sun has an unnatural quality: though it comes from a natural object, it feels artificial and constructed. It has a drug-like power to resemble "antipyrine," or to cause sleep, as it does to the "silk trees" in the second stanza.

The sun's ability to morph from one sensorial register to another is echoed in the poem's use of language from different registers, including transliterated foreign loan words ("antipyrine" [アンチピリン, *anchipirin*] and "banner" [フラフ, *furafu*] written in the script for foreign words, *katakana*), Sinified neologisms for foreign words written in Chinese characters (the word for trumpet (喇叭, *rappa*), of Dutch origin, and 万華鏡, "*hyaku megane*," for "kaleidoscope"). and many words of domestic Japanese vocabulary. The multilingual nature of this poem's vocabulary reflects Yanagawa's history of proximity to Dutch and Portuguese trading outposts in Nagasaki and Kitahara's interest in *nanban shumi*, or southern exoticism, a self-consciously exotic style found in his previous poetry collection *Heretics*, which drew inspiration from Edo-period hidden Christianity in Kyushu.[21] Just as the sun disorients the speaker's senses, it also disorients language itself, bringing to light its chaotic hybridity and its ability to morph between different national and temporal idioms.

Under the sun's intoxicating influence, the speaker holds a kaleidoscope, a proto-cinematic device. The speaker expresses a sense of personal connection to the kaleidoscope, calling it "my eerie box" (わが怪しき函, *waga ayashiki hako*), emphasizing his sense of identification with it via the possessive pronoun waga or "my," suggesting that his deepest secrets lie concealed within. The box does not only conceal; it also leaves its contents vulnerable to exposure, by virtue of the fragility of its "thin lens" (薄きレンズ, *usuki renzu*), which admits the disorienting sunlight that pervades the scene. Within the box lies the faint "magic lantern dreams" (幻燈のゆめ, *gentō no yume*), another common Meiji-period proto-cinematic attraction.[22] The proto-cinematic dreams concealed in the speaker's secret box portray "projections of a town" (街の射影, *machi no sha'ei*), suggesting Yanagawa's artificiality and mechanized quality. The speaker's inner box conceals the secret knowledge that his hometown is a mere "projection" constructed by the light of the sun.

The exposure of the contents of the speaker's secret box causes a reaction of viscerally felt corporeal anxiety, a moment of intense feeling in his "body and soul" (身と霊, *mi to tamashii*) that fills him with a "young man's awe" (少年の恐怖, *shōnen no osore*). The speaker's terror and discomfort around his physical body are triggered by the moment of exposure of his "secret," the hidden contents of his eerie box. Is the boy himself a mere "projection," like the town concealed in his kaleidoscope? The "hands of childhood" with which the speaker holds the device suggest the moment's setting in the distant past, lending it a further quality of remove and distance. The sun's light, in the first stanza an intoxicating sensory experience, now takes on a threatening, dominating quality, like the "glaring gaze of a judge" (眩き判官のまなざし, *mabayuki hangan no manazashi*), and seems to subject the speaker to the threat of surveillance, judgment, or punishment associated with the Meiji state. Aaron Gerow has written how "films were subject to censorship from the beginning" of the medium in the Meiji period.[23] Kitahara's cinematic portrayal of childhood memory in "Sun" brings in the state regulation of cinema as well, suggesting that the child's cinematically tinged inner life involves a complex interaction with the state, police, and the apparatuses of surveillance and censorship.

"Night": A Multipronged Critique of the Meiji State Involving Public Health, Time, and Cinema

In the poem "Night" (夜, "Yoru"), Kitahara uses silence and blank spaces to register the cholera epidemics that afflicted the area surrounding Yanagawa during his childhood, while also integrating a critique of the Meiji state's modernization efforts. His critique of the Meiji state takes on three realms of what it meant for the state to impose modernity on Japan: public health, the adoption of modern clock time, and police involvement in the surveillance of cinema.

Night

Night is black . . . black of the back of silver foil.
Smooth black of the beach as the tide recedes,
And then the black of the fly curtain in the theater as it falls,
The black of a ghost's hair.

Night is black . . . slimy snake's eyes shine,
tooth-blackening dye smells foul,
A pill peddler's bag loiters
Black cat walks softly. . . . night is black.

Night is black . . . black of a thief's frightening stealth.
Sadakurō's snake-eye umbrella,
Like someone unknown brushing the nape of the neck,
Like the lifeless wings of a dead firefly,

Night is black . . . eerie black numbers on the clock face.
Night when the Liver Taker[24] looks in on me,
blood dripping,
from metallic pale white scissors in his hand.
Night is black . . . . Night when I try and try to close
my eyes, but blue, red countless dead souls fall upon me.
Night when my ears are ringing, depths unknown
Dark night.
Lonely night.
night . . . night . . . night . . .

夜

夜は黒．．．．．．銀箔の裏面の黒。
滑らかな潟海の黒、
さうして芝居の下幕の黒、
幽霊の髪の黒。

夜は黒．．．．．．ぬるぬると蛇の目が光り、
おはぐろの臭いやらしく、
千金丹の鞄がうろつき、
黒猫がふわりとあるく．．．．．．夜は黒。

夜は黒......おそろしい、忍びやかな盗人(ぬすびと)の黒、
定九郎の蛇目傘(じゃのめがさ)、
誰だか頸(くび)すぢに觸(さわ)るやうな、
力のない死蛍の翅(はね)のやうな。
夜は黒......時計の数字の奇異(ふしぎ)な黒。
血潮のしたたる
生(なま)じろい鋏を持って
生胆取(いきぎもとり)のさしのぞく夜。
夜は黒......瞑(つぶ)つても瞑つても、
青い赤い無数(むすう)の霊(たましひ)の落ちかかる夜。
耳鳴(みみなり)の底知れぬ夜(よる)。

暗い夜。

ひとりぼつちの夜。

夜...夜...夜...[25]

The poem describes a series of disconnected visual images in a black-and-white color scale, suggesting the disorienting experience of visual overload associated with the new medium of cinema. Some of the poem's images recall Kabuki theater, the source material for many Meiji-period films, such as the villainous character Ono Sadakurō from the Kabuki play *Chūshingura*, or the tooth-blackening dye used by the female characters in these Edo-period dramas. In cinematically infused terms, the poem portrays the night terrors of a little boy visited by the Liver Taker (Ikigimo-Tori), a folkloric monster dating to cholera epidemics of the Meiji period. Cholera patients who died in forced hospitalization, never to return to their families, were said to have fallen victim to this creature, who removed their organs while they were still living. Tales of this creature emerged from popular fear and suspicion of modern medical treatment, often coercively imposed by the state on rural communities. In one case in Chiba Prefecture in 1877, local fishermen beat a doctor to death because of rumors that he had taken the livers of his cholera patients, like the feared "Liver Taker."[26]

The name "Liver Taker" was also applied to a serial killer called Baba Katsutarō (馬場勝太郎, circa 1875–1908), who, over a period from 1905 to 1906, cut out the internal organs of five women and children, believing that they were medical remedies for consumption.[27] The media coverage of Baba reflected popular anxiety over the state's imposition of medical advances and public health. Popular images of the Liver Taker were not just an outgrowth of superstitious fear of scientific medical advances; they were also a powerful symbol of the "popular contestation that emerged in response to the Meiji state's efforts to bring health—and its lack—under governmental control ... a series of confrontations between the government and the people over the question 'whose body is it?'"[28] The Liver Taker's appearance in the poem brings such ideological clashes between the Meiji state and the people to bear on the child's hermetic little world. *Whose dreams, whose body, and whose room is it?* the boy seems to ask himself, as his world is cast into doubt. Is his private world as safe and innocent as he thought, or are the ideological clashes taking place outside seeping in? The Liver Taker, with his roots in folklore, as well as in mass media accounts of the murder case, joins with Sadakurō and the imagery of cinematic historical dramas to create a sense of the boy's media-saturated inner life, populated by demons drawn from popular forms.

Fukasawa points out that Kitahara's well-to-do family owned a wall clock during his childhood in Yanagawa.[29] Kitahara's preface to the collection mentions that he had a childhood fear of the family clock and associated it with the tales of the Liver Taker's deadly visits to cholera wards:

> And the sound of the clock in the middle of the night marks the stealthy footsteps, dripping blood, of the Liver Taker on Tonka John's little brain,[30] numb with fevered imaginings, as if pulling him into the dark depths of time, when it strikes the hour.[31]

> 眞夜中の時計の音もまた妄想に痺れた Tonka John の小さな頭腦に生膽取の血のついた足音を忍びやかに刻みつけながら、時々深い奈落にでも引つ込むやうに、ボーンと時を點つ。

In "Night," the horrifying quality of the clock points to the constructed nature of time itself: As Stefan Tanaka has argued, clock and calendar time were an imposition of Western-influenced modernity that supplanted earlier, more heterogeneous understandings of time in Japan.[32] The "eerie black numbers on the clock face" suggest the popular anxiety that accompanied the top-down imposition of clock time as part of the Meiji state's modernization efforts. Tanaka writes how the imposition of clock and calendar time represented a paradigm shift in the everyday life of people living in Japan, whereby earlier, more heterogeneous understandings of time were replaced by the abstract, homogenous notion of capitalistic temporality.³³ Tanaka writes of the disorientation experienced by the average person whose understanding and experience of time were upended: "When the reckoning of time changes, one's very relation to the world is both disoriented and altered."³⁴ In "Night," Kitahara evokes the disorienting alteration represented by the imposition of clock time in the Meiji period.

In addition, Kitahara folds in nation-building efforts associated with cinema into the poem, via the black-and-white color scheme and the Kabuki imagery redolent of *jidai-geki* films. Gerow has written how early cinema was deeply implicated in Meiji nation-building efforts, posing the question "does the cinema merely reflect the nation or does it actually help construct it?"³⁵ By connecting the speaker's nightmares to cinema, public health, and time, Kitahara exposes the dark side of history, encouraging the reader to feel empathy for those left behind by Meiji modernization's narrative of ceaseless teleological progress and advancement.

The clock's sound pulls him down "into the dark depths of time," where he encounters the "ghosts" and "countless dead souls" in the poem, perhaps belonging to those who have fallen victim to the Liver Taker. Meanwhile, the Liver Taker "looks in on" him, with a luminous flash from his "metallic pale scissors." The flash of light calls out to the little boy and draws him in: he knows the Liver Taker is there to "look in on [him]" (さしのぞく, *sashi-nozoku*). The damaged, fragmented form of the poem, ultimately trailing off into a series of ellipses ("night . . . night . . . night . . ."), reveals how the suffering of those left behind by the Meiji state's national modernization enterprise is unspeakable; it escapes language's expressive capacity.

Like the speaker in "Sun," the boy in "Night" is confronted with dark secrets about himself, moments of self-discovery that overwhelm language's capacity to signify. These moments of unveiling are mediated by imagery drawn from visual cultures: the boy's proto-cinematic kaleidoscope in "Sun" and frightening black-and-white images suggestive of cinematic kabuki theater adaptations in "Night."

An illustration hand drawn by the poet extends Kitahara's critique of the Meiji state's imposition of clock time. This caricature of the poet as a clown accompanies a parodic rehashing of the motif of clock time in "Night." Figure 2 shows a tiny figure wrapped in puffy, voluminous clothing. Kitahara's sad clown persona draws on the character

FIGURE 1. "Yōnen no Hi," illustration, Kitahara, *Omoide*.

of Pierrot, an early Meiji-period import via Italian and French performing traditions, often associated with themes of transformation and metamorphosis, for example in the symbolist poetry of Jules Laforgue (1860–87).[36] The whimsical portrait suggests that the poet-as-clown is just a constructed, mask-like face, but somehow also vulnerable beneath the artifice.

The Pierrot's overhead thought bubble contains handwritten roman numerals, which point to the frequent use of numbered units throughout the book, in such sequences as the numbered sections of the prose preface, or the numbered sequence of poems called "Fragments." However, there is more to the numbers than just their playful, self-aware comment upon the structure of the book. The written caption beside the sequence of numerals reads, "Oh, the frightfulness of the sound of the moving clock." The numbers recall the recurring image of a ticking clock, which is a source of fear as well as fascination for the childlike speakers of the poems in *Memories*. For example, in the poem "Night," discussed earlier, the numbers of the clock are the catalyst for the child's encounter with the horrors of the past: "Night is black . . . black

FIGURE 2. "Shiba Kōkan Dōhanga," illustration, Kitahara, *Omoide*.

of the clock numbers." In the drawing, once again, the sound of time passing somehow renders the fabric of time permeable, and revenants from history appear with all the intensity of a nightmare. In the drawing, Kitahara plays on the poetic intensity of this image, undercutting it by calling attention to its constructedness. The puffy, odd little figure suggests a lighter, gently ironic perspective on the darkness of "Night."

Photography and State Power in *Memories*

In a pair of illustrations, a photograph of Yanagawa and a lithograph of pre-Meiji Edo, Kitahara extends his state critique to the realm of visual representation. First, he includes a 1784 copperplate engraving of a riverside scene in the Ochanomizu area of Edo. The image Kitahara chooses features a line of wooden warehouses and people busily milling around on one side of the river, and a line of trees on the other, with a small bridge connecting the two banks. Edo-period artist Shiba Kōkan (司馬江漢, 1747–1818), an early adopter of linear perspective who spent much of his career in and around the international port of Nagasaki, relatively near Yanagawa, uses the three-dimensional technique in this engraving: Buildings, river, and trees all stretch into the distance in three curved but parallel lines, apparently reaching into infinity. In the distant background, although it is hard to make out in the low-quality reproduction in *Memories*, there is a hazy image of Mount Fuji.[37]

Maki Fukuoka has written how Shiba Kōkan was involved in the origins of photography in Japan, as he was one of the first to use the word *shashin* (写真) to refer to images characterized by the Western-influenced technique linear perspective.[38] Fukuoka observes:

> Kōkan's approach to picture making and his uses of the term *shashin* have come to be accepted as standard for the entirety of the early modern discourse on *shashin*. Historians of Japanese photography perceive the association Kōkan made among the pictorial techniques of Western pictures, the device of the camera obscura, and the term *shashin* as a kind of originary moment that would lead more than fifty years later to the equation and conflation of photography and *shashin*.[39]

The lithograph expresses Kitahara's complex relationship to Meiji modernity. On the one hand, it evokes Shiba's eager embrace of technological progress towards the telos of modern photographic realism. On the other hand, the image's vivid portrayal of the Edo period brings a tone of nostalgia and retrospection that suggests modernity and progress may not be all they are cracked up to be. The lithograph's bustling riverside scene of commerce and human activity beside the Kanda River recalls an earlier era that predates the Meiji turn to modernity. For the city of Edo, waterways played a crucial role in transit and commerce, but by the Meiji period, Tokyo began to rely more on land-based modes of transit, like roads, streets, and railroads. Jinnai Hidenobu has written how "The history of Tokyo since the Meiji Restoration is the history of its transformation from a city on water to a city on land."[40]

I have noted how Yanagawa's canals, too, were associated with the pre-Meiji past, so that novelist Fukunaga Takehiko would later portray the town as backward and peripheral, left behind by the forward progress of linear history. So Kitahara's inclusion of Shiba's image of Edo as "a city on water" connects Yanagawa to the nation's capital. Both share a past as cities of water, which is displaced by Meiji modernity. The vague presence of Mount Fuji in the background of the Shiba engraving raises the question of Japanese national identity and its connection to landscape as mediated by visual art.

In the preface, when Kitahara describes his encounter with the engraving in a secondhand shop, the poet describes himself a rag picker illicitly savoring the storefront detritus of history and playfully assembling it into newly reconfigured forms.

> In addition, the engraving by Shiba Kōkan included in this collection is something I furtively acquired when it was abandoned in

the trash at the time of its preliminary sale at a secondhand shop, a work of curious coloring and a deeply impressive exotic quality, though the loss of the original picture's elegance due to the indistinctness of the photograph is to be regretted above all else.

なほこの集に挿[41]んだ司馬江漢の銅版畫は第一回の競賣の際古道具屋の手に依て一旦埃塵溜(ごみため)に投げ棄てられたのをそつと私の拾つて來たものであて、着色の珍らしい、印象の強い異國趣味のものだつたのが寫眞の不鮮明な爲め全く原畫の風韻を失つて了つたのはこの上もなく殘念に思はれる。[42]

Kitahara emphasizes the "exotic" (異國趣味, *ikoku-shumi*) quality of Shiba Kōkan's quintessentially Edo townscape. In so doing, he evokes the utopian longing for Edo that characterizes so much of the Pan Society's work. To long for Edo is to long for the world to be otherwise.

Interestingly, Kitahara seems to use the term "photograph" (寫眞, *shashin*) in a slightly different way from Shiba, who associated the word with the enthusiastic support of Western modernity and progress. Rather, for Kitahara in this passage, photography is associated with regret for a lost past rendered inaccessible by the passage of time and the ravages of photographic reproduction. According to Kitahara, photography seems to have drained the lithograph of its exotic, impressive quality.

Therefore, it is remarkable that Kitahara includes a photograph of Yanagawa's Okinohata River later in the collection, despite his seeming ambivalence about the damage photography can do to the past it represents.

In the prose preface, Kitahara writes of the photograph in the following terms:

People who look at the photograph of Okinohata River will feel faint waves of a kind of exotic longing at the vision of the ripples drawn in the water by the hands of a washerwoman washing the roots of a Chinese peony one midsummer day at noon in the shade of willows, sandalwood, and wax trees, while in the city's center the manmade canals' water shines bright white.

沖ノ端(おきのはた)の寫眞を見る人は柳、梅檀、櫨などのかげに、而も街の眞中(まんなか)人工的水路の、水もひたひた白く光つては芍藥の根を洗ひ洗濯女の手に波紋を畫く夏の眞晝の光景に一種のある異國趣味的情緒の微漾を感ずるであらう。[43]

FIGURE 3. Kitahara, *Omoide*.

In this passage, Kitahara connects lyric poetry's utopic longing for a different world (情緒, *jōsho*) to the transformation wrought by photography on the past. Rather than a blurry, poor-quality reproduction that detracts from the original, this photograph is an invitation to dream and yearn in vivid terms of a city of water that combines Yanagawa and Edo. He emphasizes the "manmade" quality of the canals, that they are vestiges of an earlier time when humanity interacted with landscape in a way that differed from the Meiji period's emphasis on modernity and progress.

Gyewon Kim writes how landscape photography, such as the photograph of Okinohata River in *Memories*, was implicated in Meiji nation-building efforts.[44] She writes how

> the landscape photographs that I look at here are more than just faithful reflections of the changing landscape. They function as a cultural catalyst, mediating the very transformation of the landscape as an image and as a representational form . . . Very generally, what happened to the determination of space and place in late nineteenth century Japan can be understood as part of the process of modernization; space is made commensurate with, or at least adaptable to, a new constellation of events, forces, and institutions that, taken together, came to be defined as "modernity" and progressivism.[45]

Landscape photography was also an important part of the Meiji emperor's official national tours, which included stops in Fukuoka Prefecture in 1872.⁴⁶ Kim writes how, during these imperial tours, "Photography here was employed as an embodiment of the emperor's eye"⁴⁷ such that "the emperor was implicated in a visible display of power, both by seeing his people and by being seen by them."⁴⁸ It is interesting to think of the landscape photograph of Okinohata River in relation to photography as the embodiment of the emperor's gaze. Is the poet's view of his childhood past all that different from the carefully choreographed documents of the emperor's travels? Both seek to curate landscape in accord with memory, whether that memory be that of national history, or the individual poet's recollection.

We have seen how, in the preface, Kitahara frames the photograph as a mode of lyrical longing for a lost past. The politics of this longing are potentially slippery and complex. Kitahara asks in the poem "Prelude," which opens the collection: "Is this memory, or merely our own autumn legend?" (思ひ出か、たゞし、わが秋の中古傳説?).⁴⁹ The pronoun I have translated as "our own," *waga*, has a collective ring that is often associated with the nation, as in "our country" (わが国, *waga kuni*) or "our troops" (わが軍, *waga gun*). "Our own autumn legend" therefore suggests that the poet's memories are implicated in the national narrative, the Meiji state's push for modernization and progress. Kitahara's photograph highlights the intertwining of memory (personal) and legend (national) in the poetry collection, so that the image captures at once the technological reorganization of space and time, and the poet's nostalgic yearning for a world that was displaced by the workings of state power.

The "Fragments" Sequence: Fragmentary Structures of Temporal Embeddedness

The sequence called "Fragments" adopts the point of view of a child lost in a crowd at a small-town festival. The boy wanders into a movie theater, where he feels frightened by the strange people in the audience and the images onscreen. "Fragments" portrays the dilemma of the poet seeking to take a critical position toward Japanese modernity: A lost child who wanders through a world that he finds alienating and foreign, yet also compelling and attractive. Kitahara's poems hover on the periphery of the historical phenomena they document, the way the child speaker of "Fragments" peeps into the world of adulthood and spectacle hidden behind the curtain.

35

A show on festival day, of a person's face even in the smelly
    gaslight,
from a gap in the frightening curtain, the flash of a motion
    picture looks through,
someone with cheap face powder walking within the crowd.
nevertheless, nevertheless, this helplessness of my young self,
    this flow of tears.

36

A keen, rustic whistle, and oh, my tears begin to flow.
When the chaotic motion picture is projected on a sooty cloth,
when gaslight sinks and extinguishes in a temporary tent on the
    outskirts of town,
a keen, rustic whistle, and oh, my tears begin to flow.

37

Alas, alas,
watching a blue tinted magic lantern,
why was I so forlorn as a child and cried?
Well, now I will go to a club, meet a friend,
order deep red tomato slices and call for a glass of whiskey,
to celebrate proud youthful days.

三十五
縁日の見世物の、臭き瓦斯にも面うつし、
怪しげの幕のひまより活動寫真の色は透かせど、
かくもまた廉白粉の、人込のなかもありけど、
さはいえど、さはいえど、わかき身のすべもなさ、涙ながるる。

三十六
鄙びたる鋭き呼子そをきけば涙ながるる。
いそがしき活動寫真煤びたる布に映すと、
かりそめの場末の小屋に瓦斯の火の消え落つるとき、
鄙びたる鋭き呼子そをきけば涙ながるる。

三十七
あはれ、あはれ、
色青き幻燈をみてありしとき、
なになればたづきなく、かのこども涙ながれし
いざやわれ、倶樂部にゆき、友をたずね、
紅(くれなゐ)のトマト切り、ウイスキイの酒や呼ばむ、
ほこりあるわかき日のために。[50]

Like "Sun" at the beginning of this chapter, these poems pinpoint the Meiji state as an agent of punishment and surveillance through the eyes of a young speaker participating in the modern entertainment of cinema. I have indicated that Gerow has written how "As a larger potential threat, films were subject to censorship from the very beginning."[51] To engage with cinema in poetry, then, is to engage with state involvement in its creation and regulation. At first, cinema was legally classified alongside other performing arts like theater, but in 1912, the year after *Memories* was published, cinema became its own legal category of censorship and surveillance.[52] "Fragments 35–37" provide a glimpse at the dangers and thrills of illicit entertainments including cinema.

The illicit nature of cinema relates to the status of the crowd. Gerow comments "the cinema from the start was also a medium of the body, not just of sight."[53] Cinema was dangerous in part because it brought bodies in proximity to one another in public, anonymous spaces. The speaker's immersion in a childhood memory of getting lost at a fair catalyzes a series of Proustian memory shocks with all the sensory intensity of a cinematic flashback. The impact of this memory shock connects the young boy to the crowd that surrounds him, dissolving the boundaries between himself and others. The boy finds himself immersed in an urban, collective setting, rather than the intense solitude of other poems, such as "Night."

The poems reveal the speaker's ambivalence toward the experience of existing in an urban crowd: The crowd is overwhelming and threatening to the speaker's sense of self, but it also offers thrilling new affective and aesthetic experiences. The boy is learning new perceptual and critical skills in order to participate in the spectacle of urban modernity, on the streets as well as in the cinema. Many Taishō-period writers and thinkers, such as Gonda Yasunosuke (権田保之助, 1887–1951) or Kon

Wajirō (今和次郎, 1888–1973), sought to understand modern Japan by analyzing urban Tokyo crowds, describing how crowds provided opportunities to perform new subjectivities, such as the "*moga,*" or modern girl, for example.[54] Kitahara does not document the Tokyo streets the way Gonda and Kon did. Instead, he depicts the traces it leaves on his retrospective memories of childhood. The speaker's memory, of getting lost as a child at a festival in his hometown, contains an oblique meditation on the experience of living in a crowded urban setting.

In the "Fragments" sequence, the retrospective, personal character of lyric poetry becomes a vehicle for a continual cycle of memory and shock. The past of the speaker's memory and the present of his urban Tokyo experience blur one into the other. As so often occurs in Kitahara's writing style, the poem reflects this chaotic blurring between temporalities in its mixture of words from different registers: the classical literary term あはれ, "*aware*" (alas) alongside the Meiji-era coinage "motion picture" (活動寫真, *katsudō shashin*), as well as the words "tomato" and "whiskey" of English origin.

The speaker of the poem has an unstable sense of self, one that is ready to dissolve its borders and merge with others in the crowd around him. The speaker's continual oscillation between these two registers of memory renders the "Fragments" series a disorienting sequence of conflicting shocks: The authenticity of the child speaker's immersive sense impressions is repeatedly thrown into question by the appearance of the adult speaker at a temporal remove from his child self, while the adult speaker's safe grounding in his own present is repeatedly obliterated by the overwhelming vividness of the childhood flashbacks. Who is the weeping child of the first two poems, so viscerally aware of the "helplessness" of his "young self?" Why has a fleeting glimpse of a movie playing behind a curtain catalyzed such a terrified, panicked reaction in the little boy? Why does the child of Fragments 35 and 36 feel so oddly dissociated from the first-person pronoun in Fragment 37? Most mysteriously of all, why does the adult speaker of Fragment 37 first relive the little boy's tearful panic, only to then retrospectively invest his own terrifying experience with a nostalgic glow, reminiscing drunkenly about his "proud youthful days"?

The "proud youthful days" of the childhood memory to which the adult speaker continually flashes back are themselves a moment in which the speaker's childhood self realizes his own place in the crowd and becomes part of a collective entity. The boy's forbidden gaze through the curtain returns to him with frightening intensity, as the film itself "looks through" the curtain back at the speaker. The child's glimpse of the film through the curtain in Fragment 35 is all the more "frightening" because of its forbidden, eavesdropped quality, a kind of vision he may not understand, yet knows he should not have access to. The child's glimpse of the projected world beyond the curtain becomes a realization of his own place in the crowd.

What happens once the boy finds himself enveloped by the crowd? The experience of the crowd is frightening and horrifying, yet it also has the potential for the speaker to envision himself in new ways. Looking back as an adult, the speaker remembers his "proud youthful days" with a kind of longing. The speaker goes to a club with a friend and enjoys, in the urban atmosphere of a Tokyo bar, the flashback to the anonymity of the crowd, at once terrifying and thrilling, that he experienced as a child. The "Fragments" series envisions urban modernity as terrifying, like a crowd to a small lost child, but it also explores the new experiences and modes of feeling that urban modernity has to offer. The speaker is thrust outside of himself and into a new mode of modern, collective experience, and the resulting feelings are at once thrilling and frightening. Has the boy escaped into the anonymity of an urban crowd, or into the fantasy world of a film, or both? The speaker finds himself wandering between present and past, reality and fantasy, the solitude of a lost child and the collectivity of a crowd. The crowd offers a horrifying loss of selfhood and individuality for the speaker, as well as the potential for new modes of experience among the fantastic collective of the crowd. Kitahara's poems hover on the periphery of the historical phenomena they document, the way the child speaker of "Fragments" peeps into the world of adulthood and spectacle hidden behind the curtain. It is with the charged ambivalence of an outsider who does not pretend fully to understand the phenomena he witnesses that Kitahara gives voice to his historical moment.

Kitahara's work allows us to ask what kind of poem counts as political or social critique. Is it possible to imagine a form of critically enabling poetic expression that does not explicitly position itself as such, and instead reveals its politics by its own connection to what Raymond Williams would call historically contingent structures of feeling? The little boy in "Night" makes no attempt to break free of the hermetic safety of his upper-class bedroom. The speaker of "Sun" cannot help feeling intense nostalgia for his hometown, even though he feels the intense threatening gaze of the state. The little boy in

"Fragments" is ineluctably drawn to immerse himself in the cinematic crowd despite its "frightening," threatening quality. All the poems in *Memories* partake in the same pattern: They briefly unveil some aspect of Japanese modernity, only to pull close the veil again and accept their own implication in the phenomena they have just exposed as constructed and unreal.

At times, such as in "Fragments," when the speaker takes his place in the midst of the urban crowd, there is a note of inevitability and acceptance to the "forlorn" speaker's laments in "Fragments": "Alas, alas" (あはれ、あはれ, *Aware, aware*), he exclaims. He does not actively resist his situation, or attempt to imagine any alternative. Such an active gesture would be out of place in this poem, which is too immersed in the experience it depicts to adopt the critical distance necessary to take a political stance.

The poems seem aware of their own refusal to take up the critical work they obliquely indicate. At times, such as in the fragmented ending of the poem "Night": ("Night . . . night . . . night . . ."), Kitahara's poems extinguish themselves out of self-abnegation. Yet it is by their very silence that they bear witness to the "unbearable pain" ("Sun"), left behind as the afterimage of history. Perhaps the Japanese police were oddly right to put Kitahara under surveillance in the years leading up to the publication of this work, as it is the personal realm of lyric poetry that offers potential for new kinds of politically aware imagination. This oblique model of political engagement provides a kind of blueprint for future poets who work in the realm of officially licensed state critique.

The political critiques at work in Kitahara's Meiji-period early work shifted and transformed with changes in social context, from the poet's later involvement with the Taishō-period children's poetry magazine *Red Bird* (赤い鳥, *Akai tori*), which contained critiques of what Kitahara viewed as "Western-style" children's songs that, Sawada Mayumi notes, clash with the frequent use of Western words and techniques in his own poetry, to his eventual rightward turn in the late 1930s during the Pacific War.[55] Kitahara's ability to write about childhood in *Memories* eventually made him an ideal person to transmit the "ideology of the Japanese state" to child readers in books of explicitly prowar children's poetry and songs.[56] The politics of lyric for Kitahara, an agent for decadence as well as subversive social critique in the era of the Pan Society, shifted toward the more nationalistically tinged critique of Westernization in his *Red Bird* days, before ultimately embracing the rightward nationalism of the 1930s, notably producing a song in honor of the Hitler Youth in 1938.[57] Although the nationalistic overtones of Kitahara's later works have often rendered them of marginal interest to critics, recently there have been readings by critics seeking to excavate notes of ambivalence in these later works, such as Sawada's exploration of the irony that underlies Kitahara's critiques of Westernization in *Red Bird*, or Kanno Akimasa's discussion of the dynamic interplay between vision and the unseen in Kitahara's final nationalistic *tanka* collections.[58] The half-hidden political overtones of *Memories* remain, but they become unstable and dynamic, continuing what Kitahara once called his rapid-fire, cinematic *"cut-cut-cut,"* in which hidden meanings destabilize, transform, and evade their own unveiling.

CHAPTER 2

Sexuality, Censorship, and State Critique in Hagiwara Sakutarō

This chapter shows how Hagiwara Sakutarō builds on Kitahara Hakushū's state critique in *Memories* to approach the realm of sexuality and morals. As scholars from Gregory Pflugfelder to Jim Reichert have shown, the Meiji and Taishō periods saw intense politicization and policing of sexuality in Japan as the state-imposed modernization efforts along the lines of Western-style nation states.[1] Practices of same-sex sexuality, accepted as common human behaviors during the Tokugawa period, were marginalized in favor of modern compulsory heterosexuality starting in the Meiji period. In bold, often explicit poems concerning sexuality, Hagiwara and his colleagues critique the way the state imposed compulsory heterosexuality and marginalized same-sex sexuality and other nonnormative practices. This chapter will first discuss the obscenity case related to Hagiwara's 1917 poetry collection *Howling at the Moon* (月に吠える, *Tsuki ni hoeru*). I will then examine the poet's works that appeared in minor independent magazines during this period, especially the journal *Sentiment* (感情, *Kanjō*). As we shall see, the venue of small magazines offered Hagiwara comparative freedom from state regulation and censorship in a way that his book publication did not. Together, *Howling at the Moon* and *Sentiment* offer a critique of state efforts to regulate contemporary sexual mores from the top down, and they attempt to imagine a utopic world where sexuality is open to reimagining from nonnormative perspectives.

The Poetics of Censorship in Hagiwara Sakutarō's *Howling at the Moon*

How does lyric poetry, with what Adorno calls its oblique "expression of a social antagonism," actually depend on censorship to make its point, to be effective? How have poets incorporated regulation and repression into their work? This section examines the interdependent relationship between the state and lyric poetry, where lyric criticality occupies a kind of institutionally licensed space for dissent, using the obscenity case of Hagiwara's *Howling at the Moon*. This case illustrates how lyric poetry operates in subversive ways that are also often collaborative with its own policing. Hagiwara demonstrates this in a particularly salient way in his dealings with the censors.

As Adorno argues, lyric poetry embeds its political "expression of a social antagonism" in personal, intimate subject matter. This means that poetry often ends up skirting the morality laws of the period. As we have seen in the case of the police surveillance of Kitahara's Pan Society, the line between sexual indecency and political subversion is not always straightforward and legible. While apparently an unambiguous case of obscenity, the case of Hagiwara in fact treads the line between two kinds of censorship operating in Meiji and Taishō Japan: morality standards (風俗壊乱, *fūzoku kairan*) and political order (安寧秩序, *annei chitsujo*). The line between obscenity and political subversion thus becomes somewhat blurred. In his readings of radical pornographer Umehara Hokumei (梅原北明, 1901-46), Jonathan Abel suggests that the two forms of censorship operate in tandem, and it is impossible to separate them, both from the point of view of the bureaucracy seeking to enforce them, and the cultural producers seeking to navigate them.[2] Lyric poetry, because it locates the political within the personal, offers a particularly pointed case of the blurred lines between morality and political censorship, and reveals how state power polices both these realms of daily life. As Gregory J. Kasza argues, "[t]he hazy boundary between politics and manners and morals paralleled the absence of clear demarcation between the public and private spheres," a demarcation that lyric poets like Hagiwara often blur and subvert.[3]

Japanese censorship thus blurred the lines between political and personal expression in a similar way to what poets were doing themselves in their work. Censorship itself was not a top-down, unilateral process imposed by the state on resistant artists. It was in fact a decentralized process in which state bureaucrats worked in tandem with the artists themselves, as well as with publishers and other cultural producers. Censors usually inspected publications once they were printed and available on shelves. This meant that any redactions or bans resulted in significant financial losses for the publisher and writer who had already produced the work, since the banned books or magazines were no longer saleable. To avoid these financial hits, publishers and writers collaborated closely with censors, anticipating their concerns throughout the production process. This means that the relationship between artists and censors was not necessarily antagonistic, with the courageous poet or writer resisting the repressive censorship apparatus by standing up for artistic autonomy and free speech. Rather, their relationship was very much a collaboration, in which artist and censor worked together to produce art that is acceptable in the public realm, cooperatively policing an ambiguous zone between political subversion and obscenity. *Howling at the Moon* was one of the first works to be censored under this collaborative system; though, as we shall see, there is some debate as to the nature and extent of the censorship involved.

This collaborative relationship with the censors reveals the complexity of the politics of lyric poetry, critical of the institutions it depends on for its survival. Censorship is not always an obstacle for poets to overcome: For some poets, it can help increase public notoriety and raise their public exposure. More than that, censorship can even be worked into the aesthetic structure of the poetry itself, operating as a kind of formal constraint.

One poet with a peculiarly savvy approach to navigating censorship was Hagiwara, hailed as the first to use modern vernacular Japanese (instead of classical Japanese) as a poetic language for the length of an entire volume. Not only did his early obscenity bans for *Howling at the Moon* help him to attain his prominent place in the public eye as a poet and writer, they also helped shape his poetic approach to operating in the social realm, and that of the many poets to come working under his influence.

Howling at the Moon was the first poetry collection mostly made up of poems written in modern colloquial Japanese, rather than in classical Japanese. It was and continues to be viewed as a foundational text of modern Japanese poetry. It was greatly influenced by Kitahara's *Memories*, discussed in the previous chapter, which also contained experiments with colloquial Japanese (including, as we have seen, regional dialect).⁴ *Howling at the Moon*'s influence on modern Japanese poetry would be hard to overstate. Avant-garde surrealist poet Nishiwaki Junzaburō (西脇順三郎, 1894-1982) commented that it was reading Hagiwara that made him realize for the first time that it was possible to write poetry in Japanese, and many other Japanese poets in succeeding generations have cited it as a significant influence on their work.⁵

In Hagiwara's career, *Howling at the Moon* occupies an important place as his poetic debut in what is known as the *shidan* (詩壇), or free-verse poetry community, in Japan. Previously, Hagiwara wrote *tanka*, collected in the unpublished hand-written book *Sky-Colored Flowers* (ソライロノハナ, *Sora-iro no hana*, created in 1913 and discovered and published in the 1970s). *Howling at the Moon* marks his transition to free verse, a mode of poetry writing he would pursue throughout his second major collection, *Blue Cat* (*Aoneko*, 青猫, 1923) and his third landmark book *Ice Land* (氷島, *Hyōtō*, 1934).⁶ As we shall see in chapter 4, *Ice Land* would see the poet turn away from the modern, colloquial language of *Howling at the Moon* and *Blue Cat* in favor of classically inflected linguistic elements. This retrospective turn was soon followed by Hagiwara's 1937 essay "Return to Japan" (日本への回帰, "Nihon e no kaiki"), which would later be taken up by a nationalistic coterie called the Japan Romantics (日本浪漫派, Nihon Roman-ha) as "a spiritual project of overcoming the modern and the West—thus being superior—through the nostalgic construction of a national essence."⁷ Although the essay was read and valued by Japanese nationalists, Hagiwara's own politics themselves are very complicated and much wondered about. It would be a mistake to call him a conservative or a nationalist, though his work did help inspire the Japan Romantics. The arc of Hagiwara's career begins with the experimentalism of *Howling at the Moon* and ends with the complex ambivalence of *Ice Land* and "Return to Japan." This dichotomy or dualism very much reflects the political and social turmoil of modern Japanese poetry during this period.

The censored poems in *Howling at the Moon* appear in the section of the book titled "Lonely Desire," (さびしい情慾, "Sabishii jōyoku"), the fifth of seven sections in the collection. The collection also includes two prose prefaces, one by Kitahara, thereby situating it in a lineage with his work, and the other by Hagiwara himself. The section "Lonely Desire" begins with the two censored poems, and it focuses on sexuality and its connection to psychological pain. The other six sections in the book include: "Bamboo and its Sorrow" (竹とその哀傷, "Take to sono aishō"), which uses the thin, trembling roots of bamboo as a figure for the nervous anguish of the poet; "Skylark Cuisine" (雲雀料理, "Hibari ryōri"), which uses imagery of violence and murder to explore themes of death and mortality;[8] "Sad Moonlit Night" (悲しい月夜, "Kanashii tsukiyo"), which continues the work's concern with death, inner psychology, and loneliness; "Rotten Clam" (くさつた蛤, "Kusatta hamaguri"), which uses modern scientific imagery like bacteria to represent the poet's psychological alienation; "Unfamiliar Dog" (見知らぬ犬, "Mi-shiranu inu"), which uses the collection title's image of a stray dog to represent the loneliness of urban life in early twentieth-century Tokyo; and an untitled section containing two comparatively longer prose poems. The collection as a whole weaves together its central themes of loneliness, psychological pain, violence, death, and sexuality using colloquial Japanese linguistic elements in a way that set it apart from its contemporaries.

One of the things that contributed to *Howling at the Moon*'s position as the first of something new, experimental, and modern was its initial run-in with obscenity laws immediately after its publication in 1917. According to Hagiwara's accounts, the police banned the collection for offense against morality six days after its publication, on February 21, 1917. Hagiwara received the news by telephone that day from the collection's editor, the *tanka* poet Maeda Yūgure (前田夕暮, 1883–1951), who said he had been summoned to a censor's office and told to remove the offending poems.[9] The book was then supposedly allowed back into circulation with the two most offensive poems removed by Maeda, "Sympathy" (愛憐, "Airen") and "The One Who Loved Love" (恋を恋する人, "Koi o koi suru hito"). In an essay published in the newspaper of his hometown prefecture, *Jōmō Shinbun* (上毛新聞), Hagiwara's response to the obscenity ban offers a defense of poetry as a quintessentially modern form of expression, in a way using the ban to argue for his work's place as a modern literary classic and positioning his work as "officially licensed poetry":

> If this sort of poem can be said to corrupt public morals, then at the very least, amongst the entire body of classical lyric poetry, every single one related to love should be banned. Presumably, according to this standard, the Bible's *Song of Songs*, or Japan's *Manyōshū* [万葉集] are without a doubt poems of the most extreme corruption to public morals. Why don't they ban the sale of the Bible?

I cannot help but feel a kind of ironic smile at the expression of this extraordinarily stupid fury and antipathy. To confess this sort of emotion to you all, readers, the most appropriate task would be, to print those banned . . . so-called obscene sex poems right here and let the eyes of society look upon them. However, alas, this is a task I cannot do. Those poems are forever forbidden to be printed in movable type.

Ah, what *is* poetry that corrupts public morals? This problem for me is a mystical one that cannot be guessed at. Now all I can do is express the sense that my very own poetry collection, which has just now received a revised edition, has become, to my incredibly good fortune, an officially licensed poetry collection.

若しかやうな詩編が風俗を壊乱するといふのなら、古来のあらゆる抒情詩の中でいやしくも恋愛に関するものは悉く禁されなければならない筈である。思ふにこの標準にで行くと聖書の「雅歌」や日本の「万葉集」などは最も風俗壊乱の甚だしい詩歌にちがひない。何故彼等は聖書の発売禁止を命じないか。

私はこの餘りに馬鹿馬鹿しい憤激と反感とを表現するのに一種の皮肉な微笑を感ぜずには居られない。かうした感情を読者諸君に告白するために最も適当な仕事は、その禁止されたる . . . 所謂淫猥なる色情詩なるものを茲に掲載して社会の眼で見てもらふことである。併し残念ながらその仕事は出来ないことである。その詩編は永久に活字で印刷することを禁ぜられた。

. . . ああ、風俗壊乱の詩とは何ぞ。この問題は私にとって思議することの出来ない神秘である。今はただ改版になった自分の詩集が、たいへん目出度い官許の詩集であるといふ意味のことだけを述べておく。[10]

With a sarcastic, humorous tone, Hagiwara lightheartedly pokes fun at the scandal while also using it to promote his work. He jokingly uses its supposedly explicit content to position his book on the same level as canonical works like the Bible and *Manyōshū*, and jokingly congratulates himself on having produced an "officially licensed poetry collection" now that it has been released with the offending poems removed. The humor of his tone highlights what he perceives as the absurdity of the police's decision to ban the book. It also has the effect of self-deprecating charm, whereby the poet uses the scandal to promote his work to a larger readership ("you all, readers") without seeming grandiose or like he takes himself too seriously.

Hagiwara humorously embraces his position as an "officially licensed" poet who works in tandem with the authorities, rather than posing as a free-spoken outsider who opposes them. His response thus highlights his symbiotic, collaborative relationship to censorship, rather than heroically setting himself in opposition to it. In so doing, he operates by the paradoxical logic of "officially licensed poetry," conferring legitimacy on his poetry by arguing for its place as a kind of outlaw paradoxically working within the limits of the law.

Maki Yoshiyuki points out that the reality does not quite correspond to Hagiwara's presentation of events. In the first place, *Howling at the Moon* does not appear in two major censorship archives, suggesting it was never officially banned.[11] Maki examines the "presentation copy" (納本, *nōhon*) of *Howling at the Moon*, and finds that the two offending poems had already been removed by the time the censors reviewed the text.[12] Maki suggests the most likely explanation is that Maeda Yūgure's meeting with the censors did not result in an official ban (発禁, *hakkin*), but an unofficial warning (注意, *chū'i*, or 内達, *naitatsu*), and that he had a chance to amend the text before the presentation to the censors.[13] Furthermore, Maki shows how in a March newspaper article about the case, only "Sympathy" is mentioned as needing to be removed, and "The One Who Loved Love" is not. Since the two poems are on two sides of the same series of pages, Maki suggests that "The One Who Loved Love" was not removed due to censorship, but in order to avoid reprinting the entire book.[14]

The first edition of *Howling at the Moon* eventually sent to booksellers had the problematic pages removed with scissors and replaced with a sheet of paper containing a notice that the two poems had been censored. The censorship was thus a visible part of the book's presentation, part of the impression it sought to make on readers as innovative and modern.

According to Tsuboi Hideto, the censorship notice "can be said to be one of the things that give *Howling at the Moon* its status."[15] Tsuboi emphasizes the physical reality of the book as an artifact of censorship, with its visibly missing pages and inserted notice: "Material has a life span, and it will certainly be broken and wounded, but this poetry book has the particular wound of deletion. Objects have wounds. Human bodies can also be wounded, but objects have wounds, too. It is a kind of stigma, a stigmata."[16] Tsuboi reads the censored book as a kind of wounded body, displaying the marks of its creators' collaboration with the state.

I will now explore how the bodily wounds of censorship manifest in the text itself of the deleted poems. What gaps exist in their portrayal of sexuality and the body, and how does poetic form serve to make these gaps signify? Is it precisely through the wounds inflicted by censorship, self-imposed or otherwise, that these poems make their political and social critiques?

"Sympathy:" Plant Sexuality as Smokescreen

The collection's engagement with censorship is crucial to understanding its place as a foundational text in modern Japanese poetry. For example, the deleted poem "Sympathy" uses plant imagery and metaphor to obliquely depict scenes of sexuality, thereby incorporating a kind of "officially licensed" aesthetic into its form and content. The poem depicts a scene of "snake-like play" (蛇のやうなあそび, *hebi no yō na asobi*), an indirect way of referring to masturbation. The poem explicitly refers to the woman's "breasts" (乳房, *chibusa*), depictions of which are not illegal; however it obliquely evokes the more heavily policed images of pubic hair and genitals using the image of grass and bellflowers:

Sympathy
Bite down hard with your strong, adorable teeth,
You, woman, bite down on the green of the grass,
Woman,
With the pale green of the grass juice,
I will color your face all over,
Exciting your desire,
We shall play in the thick grass in secret
Look,
The bellflowers shake their heads
And gentians softly move their hands right *there*
Ah, I hold your breasts firmly
You, with all your strength, press yourself down on my body
Doing so in this deserted field,
We will play like snakes
Ah, I grind into you with my body,
On your beautiful skin I spread the juice of green grass.

愛憐

きつと可愛いかたい歯で、
草のみどりをかみしめる女よ、
女よ、
このうす青い草のいんきで、

まんべんなくお前の顔をいろどつて、
おまへの情慾をたかぶらしめ、
しげる草むらでこつそりあそばう、
みたまへ、
ここにはつりがね草がくびをふり、
あそこではりんだうの手がしなしなと動いてゐる、

ああわたしはしつかりとお前の乳房を抱きしめる、
お前はお前で力いつぱいに私のからだを押へつける、
さうしてこの人気のない野原の中で、
わたしたちは蛇のやうなあそびをしよう、
ああ私は私できりきりとお前を可愛がつてやり、
おまへの美しい皮膚の上に、
青い草の葉の汁をぬりつけてやる。[17]

The poem uses botanical language to obscure the sexual acts taking place, but also to heighten the eroticism of the scene.[18] The "hands" of the gentian flowers "right *there*" (あそこでは, *asoko de wa*), as well as the verbs "move" (動いてゐる, *ugoiteiru*) and "play" (あそびをしよう, *asobi o shiyō*) suggest digital stimulation and masturbation. The term あそこ, "*asoko*" (over there), is sometimes used to refer to genitals (somewhat like "down there" in English), and the use of the compound particle では ("*de wa*") marks "*asoko*" as the location of action, as well as the topic of the sentence, emphasizing that the hands of the flowers are playing in a masturbatory manner.

Howling at the Moon's illustrations serve both to highlight and obscure the explicit quality of the imagery. The illustrations were by Tanaka Kyōkichi (田中恭吉, 1892–1915) and Onchi Kōshirō (恩地孝四郎, 1891–1955), two creative printmaking (創作版画, *sōsaku hanga*) artists affiliated with the decadent, art-for-art's-sake visual arts coterie Moon's Radiance (月映, Tsuku-hae). Onchi had collaborated with Hagiwara previously in work for the poetry journal *Sentiment* (感情, *Kanjō*, 1916–19), and it was through him that Hagiwara approached Tanaka. The book's visual design was highly praised at the time of its release, with Kitahara commenting, "What excellence! I'm completely dazzled.

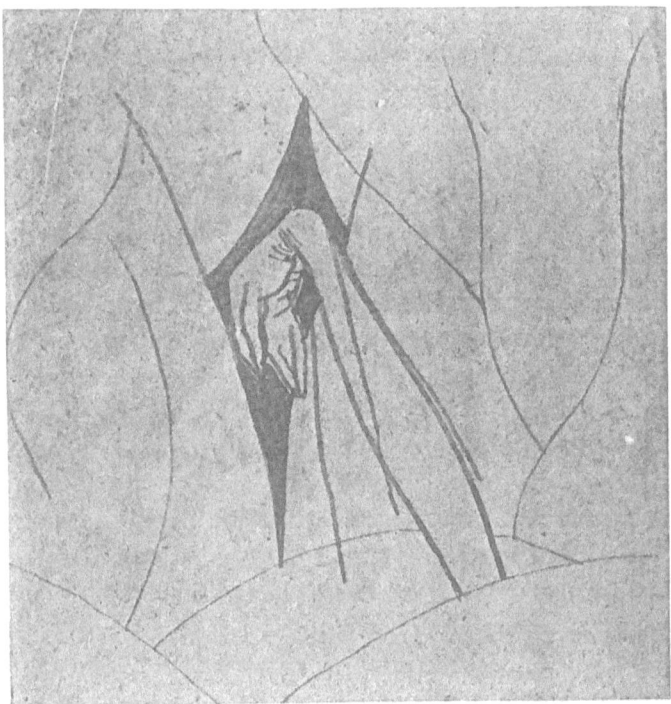

FIGURE 4. Tanaka Kyōkichi, "Study 1," illustration from first edition of *Howling at the Moon*, reprinted in Hagiwara Sakutarō, *Howling at the Moon and Other Poems by Hagiwara Sakutarō*, trans. Hiroaki Sato (University of Tokyo Press, 1978). Owned by the Museum of Modern Art, Wakayama

I knew about the content, but what about that book design! Tanaka Kyōkichi is so talented. You found the right person. I can tell this is someone who creates images that fit with your poetry."[19] Hagiwara would cite the fin de siècle decadent illustrator Aubrey Beardsley's work for Oscar Wilde's *Salome* as an inspiration.[20] Three of the illustrations, including the one featured above, were pen drawings on the pink paper that contained Tanaka's tuberculosis medication. Tanaka would die in October 1915 before the release of the collection.

In the illustration above, a close-up of a flower suggests folds of labia and perhaps a finger or a hand. Portrayals of nudes in poetry publications were highly policed starting with the banning of the poetry magazine *Morning Star* in November 1900 for an illustration depicting a female nude (previous covers of the magazine featuring only nude busts were permitted; it was only once the magazine featured a full-length nude, with a suggestive but very minimal rendering of a vagina, that the police intervened).²¹ The visual portrayal of nudes was thus illegal, but Hagiwara reveals that by using indirect, suggestive imagery, the words of the poem can compensate for what is left out of the illustrations. Indeed, the ambiguity of the scene can be said to heighten the eroticism by stimulating the reader to participate using his or her imagination.

The repeated use of the intimate, informal second-person pronoun *omae* (お前) emphasizes the connection and intimacy between the two characters. It also gives the addressee a sense of active participation in the scene: *Omae* is the grammatical topic of the sentence, so that she is positioned on top of the poem's syntax, a kind of momentary reversal of the rest of the poem, whose grammatical subject is either "I" (私, *watashi*), or an implied first-person plural ("let us play," あそびをしよう, *asobi o shiyō*).

Sexualizing plant life was part of Hagiwara's poetic practice, pushing the bounds of normative, accepted sexual acts beyond the realm of human beings. Dean A. Brink argues that Hagiwara's plant imagery anticipates ecological concerns of the Anthropocene, creating a postnatural world in which nonhuman beings have agency.²² Tamura Keiji shows that the term "plant fornication" (草木姦淫, *sōmoku kan'in*) appears as a key motif in Hagiwara's personal letters from this period: "I perceived that, one night, with 'the kind of pain that melts flesh,' I fornicated with the seed of plants," Hagiwara wrote in a letter to his cousin Hagiwara Eiji (萩原栄次).²³ Plant sexuality allowed him to experiment with "the kind of pain that melts flesh," blurring boundaries between human flesh and plant environment, and between pain and pleasure.

As we have seen, there is a fluid quality to the poem, in which distinctions between male and female, genitals and plant life, speaker and addressee, tend to blur together. This blurring of boundaries has a smoke screen effect, allowing the poem to skirt obscenity laws that regulate more explicit depictions of sexuality. However, was it possible that Hagiwara went too far with his smokescreen? Perhaps the fluidity and ambiguity with which he describes the sex scene creates a more perverse, obscene reading experience, by engaging the reader's imagination as an active participant. Perhaps a full-on nude love scene would have been less obscene than the plant-obscured ambiguity of the poem, in which it is not always possible to tell who is doing precisely what to whom, but the very obscurity of the poem invites speculation.

"The One Who Loves Love": Androgyny, Masculinity, and Literary Imitation of the West

The other banned poem, "The One who Loves Love," contains a non-normative, androgynous depiction of masculinity, describing a masculine speaker cross-dressing in feminine clothing and makeup. In unexpurgated editions of *Howling at the Moon*, "The One who Loves Love" appears directly after "Sympathy," lending a kind of androgyny or fluidity to the sexual acts depicted there. Perhaps the "woman" addressed by the presumably male speaker of "Sympathy" is a gender-fluid figure playing the role of femininity.

The One Who Loves Love

I paint crimson on my lips,
I kissed the trunk of the fresh white birch,
Even if I were an attractive man,
My chest, no breasts like rubber balls.
My skin, no smell of fine, white pressed powder,
I am a shriveled, ill-fated man,
Ah, what a pathetic man I am
In today's fragrant early summer meadow
Among the glittering grove of trees,
I put
Sky-blue gloves on my hands,
I put something like a corset around my waist,
I paint something like pressed white powder all around my neck,
Thus I play the coquette in silence,
Like young girls do,
Tilting my head slightly,
I kissed the trunk of the fresh white birch,
With my lips colored deep rose,
Clung to the pure white tall tree.

恋を恋する人

わたしはくちびるにべにをぬつて、
あたらしい白樺の幹に接吻した、
よしんば私が美男であらうとも、
わたしの胸にはごむまりのやうな乳房がない、

わたしの皮膚からはきめのこまかい粉おしろいのにほひがしない、
わたしはしなびきつた薄命男だ、
ああ、なんといふいぢらしい男だ、
けふのかぐはしい初夏の野原で、
きらきらする木立の中で、
手には空色の手ぶくろをすつぽりとはめてみた、
腰にはこるせつとのやうなものをはめてみた、
襟には襟おしろいのやうなものをぬりつけた、
かうしてひつそりとしなをつくりながら、
わたしは娘たちのするやうに、
こころもちくびをかしげて、
あたらしい白樺の幹に接吻した、
くちびるにばらいろのべにをぬつて、
まつしろの高い樹木にすがりついた。[24]

The poem portrays a speaker in the midst of a gender-bending act of dress-up, using a mishmash of clothing and cosmetics from geographical and temporal settings. Sky-blue gloves, and "something like a corset" both suggest dressy, old-fashioned Western style women's clothing, something worn to a ball or in a play at the theater. The speaker's choice in makeup recalls Edo-period Japanese beauty practices, such as his use of *o-shiroi*, white makeup powder, not only on his face, but on his neck. It is worth noting that the feminized, androgynous kind of masculinity performed in this poem draws on a long, conventional lineage in Japan, the practice of male actors playing women on the Kabuki stage, *onna-gata*. However, starting in 1872, cross-dressing outside of the theater was illegal, meaning that the speaker is breaking the law.

The presumably male speaker deprecates his own manhood, referring to himself as a "pathetic man." He is therefore coded as male, but as a kind of beta-male, who sees himself as pitiful and lacking. He seems to revel in this lack of manliness: he indulges in feminine clothing and Edo-inflected cosmetics. The speaker combines self-deprecating language about his manhood with a sense of pleasure and enjoyment, as he performs femininity for his own amusement and arousal: "Thus I play the coquette in silence,/Like young girls do,/Tilting my head slightly." Here he seems to be playing both the parts from "Sympathy": the masculine speaker and the feminine addressee, and "play[s] the coquette" with himself.

The exploration of nonnormative masculinity might have been enough to draw the attention of the police; however Hagiwara adds to the obscenity by once again obliquely equating plant life and sexual organs. Here, the speaker kisses and embraces the trunk of a phallic white birch tree, giving an undercurrent of homoeroticism to the poem.

Reichert argues that male-male homosexuality was central to the development of modern Japanese literature, operating as an Other against which the heterosexual male narrator of most Japanese literature defined himself. The poem seems to be alluding to the homoeroticism and androgynous masculinity found in Japanese literary circles, poking holes in the façade of heterosexuality that occupied a central place in Japanese letters.

The white birch tree embraced by the speaker may be a reference to a literary group called the Shirakaba-ha, or White Birch Society, which was active in the 1910s, and whose most famous members included the novelists Shiga Naoya (志賀直哉, 1883-1971) and Arishima Takeo (有島武郎, 1878-1923). The White Birch writers were interested in creating utopian literary and artistic communities loosely inspired by Leo Tolstoy. They believed in idealism and the use of art to perfect the individual. Not only was Hagiwara not a member of the White Birch Society, but he also had a rather dismissive attitude toward them. As he commented looking back in 1935: "With the simple sentimentality of idealism, they worshipped the two authors [Dostoevsky and Tolstoy] without distinguishing between them, and the heroism of Shirakaba-ha seemed childish and superficial."[25] Perhaps the poem is actually a dig at what Hagiwara called the "childish and superficial" quality of Shirakaba-ha: They are imitative, playing dress-up in a naïve childish way and worshipping the Western authors they imitate. The poem's speaker seems more concerned with pleasure and fantasy than with the lofty ideals of humanism espoused by the literary society.

The title is also a possible literary reference to a short story from 1907 by the Meiji-period author Kunikida Doppo, who transitioned toward the end of his life from romantic poetry to naturalist fiction. Kunikida's "The One Who Loved Love," like Hagiwara's poem, describes the oblique homoeroticism and androgynous masculinity found in Japanese literary circles. The story depicts the missed opportunities for romantic love between a group of intellectual, literary young men and the young women they meet at a hot springs resort. At one point, one of the young protagonists, named Ōtomo, offers the following meditation on the notion of "one who loves love," in relation to his unconsummated relationship with a young woman called O-Shō:

> Ōtomo realized for the first time that O-Shō was in love with him, and then that when he longed to see O-Shō, it meant something different from when O-Shō longed to see him. He was O-Shō's beloved, but she was not his; she was just the one who offered him tears of tenderness out of compassion for his love. And he realized that he himself was only someone who loved love.

> 大友は初めてお正が自分を恋していたのを知った、そして自分がお正に会いたいと思うのと、お正が自分に会いたいと願うのとは意味が違うと感じた。自分はお正の恋人であるがお正は自分の恋人でない、ただ自分の恋に深い同情を寄せて泣いてくれた柔しサを恋したのだ。そして自分は恋を恋する人に過ぎないと知った。[26]

Here the young narrator identifies himself as someone who loves love as an abstract concept and is therefore incapable of reciprocating the more personal, concrete sentiments of someone who loves him as a person. The narrator seems to be caught in a world of abstraction, where he discusses complex ideas with his male friends, but cannot connect on a deep emotional level with anyone. Being "in love with love" seems like a lonely, isolating experience. He seems very much to fit with Reichert's argument about Meiji men of letters, who, in order to construct themselves as heterosexual male subjects, must affirm the homosocial ties between men while disavowing any homoerotic undercurrent. The young man is incapable of loving the female protagonists of the story, and he is forbidden to explicitly admit to loving any of the male protagonists. Therefore, all that is left to him is to avow himself "in love with love," thereby opting out of actively expressing his sexuality altogether in favor of living in a world of abstract thought.

Hagiwara's allusion to this story and to the White Birch Society in these sexually explicit poems could mean he is trying to reinject sexuality into the sexually repressed realm of Japanese literature, lamenting what is lost in this repressive mode of literary subjectivity, an ode to the pleasure of explicit sex acts in a realm where they are only permitted to be described obliquely. As an "officially licensed" poetry collection, *Howling at the Moon* gives voice to what has been repressed from modern Japanese literature, including homoeroticism and nonnormative male gender expression, but within a proscribed realm.[27] The poems balance explicit sexuality with the need to maintain a proscribed realm of licensed free expression.

"Murder Case": The Poet as Detective and Criminal

In a poem inspired by crime films, Hagiwara positions the poet as both criminal and police, surveilling himself, an ambiguous figure similar to the "officially licensed" poet who polices himself even as he attempts to subvert state norms. These poems draw on censorship debates of the time about crime films, which were the first films to be systematically censored in Japan. The poet portrays himself as a liminal presence, on both sides, the outlaw's and the state's, a practitioner of officially licensed state critique.

The poem is commonly thought to be inspired by the popular *Zigomar* crime films, directed by French filmmaker Victorin Jasset (1862-1913).[28] In 1910, *Zigomar* was the first film to be banned by the Tokyo police. According to Aaron Gerow, "[t]he *Zigomar* incident" was a watershed moment in Japanese censorship that "helped define a central problem with the motion pictures that authorities and social leaders would confront for some time: how to control an alluring visual (and sometimes physical) mode of signification—one that resisted the regulation of the written or spoken word—and its spectatorship."[29] Hagiwara's poem on *Zigomar* and its popular follow-up *Protea* (1913) present an ambivalent view of this watershed moment, at once skeptical of state regulation of free expression and complicit with it.

The poem "Murder Case" describes a murder in which lines between perpetrator, detective, victim, and witness all blur ambiguously. This moral gray zone reflects the fraught, collaborative nature of censorship, in which poet and censor work together to regulate the text.

Murder Case
Pistol rings out in a distant sky.
Again the pistol rings out.
Ah, my detective wears garments of glass,
Sneaking from the lover's window,
The floor is crystal,
From the space between each finger
Flows pure blue blood,
Over the sad woman's corpse,

A cold grasshopper is crying.
Morning at the start of the frosty month,
A detective in his garments of glass,
He turned at the city crossroads.
At the city crossroads, by the autumn fountain,
Now alone, the detective feels sorrow.
Look, over distant, lonely marble streets,
The suspect glides at top speed.

殺人事件
とほい空でぴすとるが鳴る。
またぴすとるが鳴る。
ああ私の探偵は玻璃の衣裳をきて、
こひびとの窓からしのびこむ、
床は晶玉、
ゆびとゆびとのあひだから、
まつさをの血がながれてゐる、
かなしい女の屍體のうへで、
つめたいきりぎりすが鳴いてゐる。
しもつき上旬(はじめ)のある朝、
探偵は玻璃の衣裳をきて、
街の十字巷路(よつつじ)を曲つた。
十字巷路に秋のふんする、
はやひとり探偵はうれひをかんず。
みよ、遠いさびしい大理石の歩道を、
曲者(くせもの)はいつさんにすべつてゆく。[30]

The poem first appeared in the inaugural issue of Kitahara's poetry journal *Earthly Pilgrimages* (地上巡礼, *Chijō junrei*), which Kitahara edited from 1914 to 1915. In the magazine, the date August 12, 1914, is given. Kitahara founded *Earthly Pilgrimages* after moving back to Tokyo for the first time since his imprisonment for adultery in 1912. Hagiwara's poem marks his contribution to Kitahara's new venture after the terrible experience. Shibusawa Takasuke even hypothesizes that the focus on law, punishment, and sin found in this and other poems Hagiwara published in the journal was in part inspired by Kitahara's ordeal.[31]

In "Murder Case," the agent of the state, the detective, is described in suspicious terms, wearing transparent "garments of glass," rather than a police uniform. The garment of glass is transparent, presumably revealing the body underneath and displaying the detective as a corporeal, bodily being with sexual and physical needs, rather than an impartial agent of justice. The glass garment is also breakable and delicate, gesturing to the fragile nature of police authority, which is vulnerable to shocks that might shatter it.

The exposed, fragile detective behaves more like a criminal than a police agent. He "sneaks" (しのびこむ, *shinobi-komu*) from his lover's window, leaving a crime scene behind him. The victim's body lies on a crystal floor, which mirrors the glass clothing of the detective, as though he is part of the crime scene.

Meanwhile, the grasshopper cries, rendering the scene elegant and poetic, since the grasshopper is a common device in classical poetry whose cries indicate melancholy, autumn, and the transience of life. Is the grasshopper a disturbing example of poetry's power to aestheticize violent acts like murder? Or is it an attempt to elevate the vulgar tropes of crime fiction with a device from canonical poetry? Regardless, the grasshopper's elegant, courtly beauty provides a kind of smokescreen or alibi for the violence of the murder.

The detective is not an impartial crime solver. Instead, he "feels sorrow" (うれひをかんず, *urei o kanzu*), mourning his dead lover. In mourning her, he aestheticizes her and renders her into poetic language, the elegant, classicized phrase "feels sorrow." Poetry is thus implicated in the detective's complicity with the crime: Like a poet, he mourns the death, but he also renders it beautiful. He does not seem particularly interested in solving the crime, but only in experiencing it as an aesthetic object through the elegant language and images of classical poetry.

At the end of the poem, a "suspect" (曲者, *kusemono*) runs away into the cityscape, leaving more questions than answers behind. What is the relationship of the detective to the suspect? Why does he only urge himself to "look" (みよ, *miyo*) at the strange figure, rather than trying to catch them or at least calling out? The distinction between detective and suspect blurs at the end of the poem, and readers are left unsure of where we stand. Do readers desire the detective to catch the suspect, or do their hearts belong to the suspect as he glides over the marble streets?

The poem's moral ambiguity recalls the censorship debates that surrounded the film *Zigomar* in 1910. As the *Asahi Shinbun* newspaper commented, "in the minds of the audiences who were watching the changes appear before their eyes on screen, no sense arose of good being rewarded and evil being punished."³² The poem "Murder Case" uses poetic language to get away with portraying the very same things that, in a filmic representation, were banned. Like "Sympathy," which used plant imagery to portray sex acts and body parts that would have been illegal in more explicit terms, "Murder Case" portrays the same blurred moral universe that got a more explicit portrayal banned. The elegant, literary quality of the language, and imagery like the grasshopper's cries, serve as smokescreens to obscure the unsavory quality of the content.

Formally, too, with the quick transitions between images, there are echoes of the fast editing style that made the *Zigomar* films a hit with audiences. As Gerow explains, it was more than the content that was in play in the film's ban. The medium of cinema itself was at issue, as fundamentally more harmful to audiences than the written word: "there was increasing concern that the motion pictures were fundamentally different from the linguistic arts."³³

Hagiwara's fascination with Jasset's *Zigomar* films also had to do with his interest in nonnormative gender presentation, which we have seen in "The One Who Loves Love." The only specified gender in "Murder Case" is that of the victim, who is a woman. Both the detective and the suspect are presented in ambiguous, unmarked terms. While the unmarked is often presumed male, the glass garments do not fit with human clothing of either gender, instead creating a figure who is liminal and difficult to categorize. The protagonist in *Protea*, Hagiwara's favorite Jasset film, is a woman whose talents include disguising herself as members of either gender. The liminal, slippery detective, who merges with the crystalline environment of the crime scene like camouflage, seems like a possible homage to Protea, who is equally at home dressing up as a male soldier or a female femme fatale. Hagiwara used the name Protea as an alias in communications with his friend the poet Murō Saisei (室生犀星, 1889–1962), suggesting that he identified with the character.³⁴

In "Murder Case," Hagiwara writes in the gap between the written word and cinema, portraying what would have been banned were it on the screen. The ambiguity of gender, the sensory overload of rapid cinematic editing, and the moral blurring between detective and perpetrator were all hot-button issues in the censorship debates surrounding *Zigomar*. In so doing, Hagiwara reveals the "officially licensed" nature of lyric poetry, where dissent and obscenity are permitted even as they are policed. In the proscribed realm of "officially licensed poetry," there exist possibilities for formal and poetic experimentation with the very limits imposed by censorship.

Throughout *Howling at the Moon*, the poet becomes a liminal figure who can be criminal or detective, man or woman, victim or perpetrator, plant or human. *Howling at the Moon* might seem like it depicts a lawless world where anything is possible, but its engagement with censorship reveals that it actually maintains strict limits and boundaries that it relies on for its transgressions to become legible. Hagiwara's liminal characters blur boundaries and subvert accepted norms around morality and sexuality, but all within the "officially licensed" realm of censored poetry. Hagiwara sets the precedent for the other poets in this study, incorporating censorship into the form and content of his poetry. Instead of an oppositional figure insisting on free expression against the state, Hagiwara reveals how the poet operates as a collaborator with his own regulation. Lyric poetry in Japan of this period operates in the realm between resistance and complicity, the "officially licensed" space of managed dissent.

Homoeroticism, Nationalism, and Cinema in *Sentiment* (1916–19)

Hagiwara's poems like "Murder Case" show how he used motifs drawn from cinema to create his own comments on political issues, including censorship. In the following section, I explore Hagiwara's involvement with the journal *Sentiment*. In poems featuring his close relationship with Murō, Hagiwara imagines a brotherhood of poets drawn together by a shared love of cinema and an imperialistically tinged sense of national mission. During these years, Hagiwara and Murō imagine themselves as voices of an imperialistic mission bound by ties of love and companionship. They comment in their poetry upon a series of social and political issues: the repressed homoeroticism of modern Japanese poetry, modern poetry's vexed relationship to cinema and to mass culture, and Japan's intensifying imperial endeavors overseas.

These poets' political undertones intensify in legibility if we readers look at them in the context of the small magazine in which they first appeared. As Cary Nelson remarks about avant-garde American poetry, "In reading journals one can begin to recognize the strategic, dialectical, and exclusionary relations between poetry and the other discourses of the time . . . It is actually impossible to judge what kind of discursive terrain poetry occupied, what social, political, and aesthetic functions it served, if one only reads it in anthologies and books of poems."[35]

The journal *Sentiment* was started in 1916 by Hagiwara and Murō. It ran for a total of thirty-two issues over three years from 1916 to 1919. At the time, little magazines were the foremost vehicle for modern poetry in Japan, especially in the cultural and economic center of Tokyo. Little magazines were the vehicles for new poetic ideas and experiments in poetic form. They were also the vehicles for interpersonal relationships, serving as the social glue that kept together the cliquish, coterie-based world of Japanese poetry.

> These little magazines were defined by a vexed relationship to a larger, "mainstream" public and an equally vexed relationship to money . . . [L]ittle magazines are non-commercial enterprises founded by individuals or small groups intent upon publishing the experimental works or radical opinions of untried, unpopular, or under-represented writers. Defying mainstream tastes and conventions, some little magazines aim to uphold higher artistic and intellectual standards than their commercial counterparts . . .[36]

In the Japanese poetry world or *shidan*, little magazines existed in a "vexed relationship" to an emerging concept of mainstream commercial literature, represented by the term mass literature (大衆文学, *taishū bungaku*). These small magazines are fascinating artifacts of their creators' ambivalence toward the mass media. Obviously, they would not exist if it were not for these poets' need for an alternative to more mainstream media outlets, but at the same time, they provide clear evidence of the writers' love for mass media such as film. These journals were the social glue that kept the Japanese poetry scene together, and they were sometimes their contributors' stepping-stones to more mainstream outlets. Even as these journals positioned themselves as independent alternatives, they were also deeply connected to the mass media. They were sold at bookstores, mostly in Tokyo, and met with limited circulation among educated, intellectual readers. In these independent coterie publications, poets appropriate and transform elements of the mass media, expressing their ambivalence. In their inventive appropriation of the media flow, these independently published poems address their social and political contexts in language that is steeped in the vernacular of mass culture.

Hagiwara's relationships with other poets and with the poetry world were mediated in large part by these little magazines. In 1913, the small poetry magazine *Pomelo* (朱欒, *Zanboa*), which ran from 1911 to 1913 and was edited by Kitahara, featured poems by Hagiwara and Murō. This publication in a small magazine was the occasion for forging a lifelong friendship among the three poets Hagiwara, Murō, and Kitahara. Murō and Hagiwara founded a short-lived little magazine together with the poet Yamamura Bochō (山村暮鳥, 1884–1924) called *Tabletop Fountain* (卓上噴水, *Takujō funsui*) in 1915 before moving on to *Sentiment* in 1916.

The group of poets that eventually coalesced around the journal *Sentiment*, including Hagiwara and Murō, as well as Kitahara and Takamura Kōtarō (高村光太郎, 1883–1956) were known as the Sentimental Poetry Coterie (感情詩派, *kanjōshi-ha*).[37] They are often described in opposition to another group of poets, the People's Poetry Coterie (民衆詩派, Minshūshi-ha), "which advocated the use of a plain colloquial diction that would appeal to the masses."[38] The People's Poetry Coterie, which included the poets Shirotori Seigo (白鳥省吾, 1890–1973) and Momota Sōji (百田宗治, 1893–1955), advocated for plain, colloquial poetry that addressed contemporary social issues, while the Sentimental Poetry Coterie advocated for more aesthetically focused poetry that expressed the inner emotions of the poet.

At the beginning of its three-year run, *Sentiment* was a two-man operation run by Hagiwara and Murō. Hagiwara thought of the name *Sentiment*.[39] He contributed from his home in the provincial town of Maebashi in Gunma Prefecture, while Tokyo-based Murō took care of most of the logistical day-to-day business of running the journal. The magazine was printed out of Murō's Tokyo home, and when he moved, so did the journal's headquarters.[40] The circulation was small at two hundred copies, costing a total of sixteen or seventeen yen, which Hagiwara provided himself.[41] Murō was in charge of distribution, conveying copies to the poets' friends and acquaintances as well as to Tokyo bookstores.[42]

In its earliest form, *Sentiment* was an intimate "magazine for two" (二人雑誌, *futari zasshi*).[43] The two poet-editors' relationship was intense and close. The early issues of *Sentiment* contain only the two poets' works, so it serves as a record or a memorial of their friendship. As the journal progressed, more poets published their work in it, and it became less of a dialogue between Hagiwara and Murō and more of a record of the coterie. Hagiwara withdrew his involvement toward the end of the journal in 1919, and Murō took on the editing duties himself.

From its inception, *Sentiment* lived up to its title in that it offered a heartfelt defense of feeling and passionate intensity by the two poets.

Hagiwara's choice of the name was likely connected to the overwhelming importance of emotion both in his work and in the literary scene of the period. As Jon Holt argues, a constellation of words for emotion and feeling became key terms for Hagiwara in the 1910s, including the English word "sentimental" and its Japanese glosses, *kanshō* (感傷) and *kanjō* (感情).[44] In 1918, toward the end of Hagiwara's involvement in the magazine, cover images started to feature the English word *Sentiment* in bold block letters as a subtitle and translation for *Kanjō*.

This emotion was almost always shared by the two men in a homosocial fashion, and it was frequently mediated through cinema. In Hagiwara's long poem "One Who Chases Rainbows" (虹を追ふひと, *Niji o ou hito*, 1916), published in the first issue of *Sentiment*, he uses cinematic techniques to express a homoerotic poetics of imperialist emotion.

One Who Chases Rainbows

Part 1

Place: A great plain that looks like western China.
Time: A time when these facts presumably took place.
(dialogue between two travelers wandering the great plain)

1

"How far should we go?"
"We should just go as far as we can."
"As far as we can go."
"We must keep walking until the day our duty is fulfilled."
"Do you still believe in *that*?"
"Yes."
"Do you really believe? In that foolish fairytale?"
"But you once told me that tale! And besides, you believed it!"
"I may have, long ago. For I was just a child. Children sincerely believe whatever foolish stories they hear."
"Anyway, we must fulfill our duty. We must walk even a step further before day ends."

虹を追ふひと

第一編

場。支那の西方にあるらしく思はるる大平原。

時。この事實のあったと思はるるころ。
（曠野を漂泊する二人の旅人の對話）

1
「おれたちはどこまで行けばいいのだ。
「行くところまで行くばかりだ。
「行くところまでとは
「おれたちの義務が果たされる日までおれたちは歩いて居な
　ければならない。
「君はまだあれを信じて居るのか。
「さうだ。
「ほんとに信じて居るのか。あんな馬鹿氣きった昔話を。
「でも君はいつかあの話をおれにしてくれたぢゃないか。そ
　して君はそれを信じて居たぢゃないか。
「ずっと前にはそんなこともあったやうだ。おれはほんの子
　供だったからな。子供はどんなとぼけた作り話でも本氣に
　するものだ。
「とにかくおれたちは義務を果たさなければならない。日の
　暮れないうちに一足でもよけいに歩かなければならない。[45]

Cinema is evoked by the dialogue-heavy form of the poem, which reads like a film scenario. Read in context with Hagiwara's close, intense friendship with Murō, the poem describes a homoerotic relationship based on cinema, poetry, and nationalist sentiment. It sums up the two poets' literary enterprise in their new journal *Sentiment*.

The poem is set in the wide, open space of mainland China, thereby evoking Japanese imperialist ambitions on the continent. The landscape is described as "broad" (曠野, *kōya*) and the "great plains" (大平原, *daiheigen*), suggesting its openness and potential to be traveled upon and occupied. Toshiko Ellis writes of modernist Japanese poets' fascination with Asia:

> "Asia" appeared to them as imaginary land sufficiently unknown and vaguely defined, and furthermore as a new frontier that belonged neither to Japan nor to the West. The fact that it was not an empty land waiting to be cultivated but that the Japanese intrusion meant in many cases the forced removal of indigenous people and traditional cultures is not directly taken up and problematized in the texts. In fact, [poets] stressed the vastness and emptiness of the continental "desert" in their poetic representations.[46]

Like the modernists who would follow in about a decade, Hagiwara in *Sentiment* imagines Asia as a broad, empty expanse characterized by "vastness and emptiness."

The dialogue between the two travelers emphasizes homosocial bonding between men. The pronouns, including *ore* (おれ) and *oretachi* (おれたち), emphatically mark the speakers as male. Their intimacy is represented by the use of plain form Japanese sentence endings, rather than more formal *desu–masu* endings.

In the second scene, one traveler laments to the other:

> Your heart is unknown to me. The same way we don't know our emperor's [陛下] heart. No, maybe it is even more unknown. His Highness is a true madman. But, you . . . you are alright, aren't you?
>
> おれにはお前の心がわからない。おれたちの陛下のお心がわからないやうに。いや、ことによるともっと解らない。陛下は本物の氣狂ひだ。併しおまへは．．．。おまへは大丈夫だらうな。⁴⁷

The line "[y]our heart is unknown to me" creates a sense of thwarted intimacy between the two men, as if one wants to be closer than the other is willing to go. It seems that the homosocial bond between men only goes so far, and its failure to go further engenders a sense of loneliness in one of the speakers.

The poem is set in explicitly imperialist terms, with allusions to an emperor who may or may not be mad overseeing the travelers' endeavor. The emperor's madness refers to rumors about the mental fitness of the Taishō emperor (1879–1926). The madness of the Taishō emperor was a taboo topic, unnamable outside the marginal, under-the-radar realm of little magazines like *Sentiment*. Had this reference to the "mad emperor" appeared in a more mainstream journal, it would undoubtedly have incurred a response from the censors. This potentially provocative phrase recalls what Hagiwara would later say about being an "officially licensed" poet who can express taboo sentiments in a proscribed realm.

In sum, the poem "One Who Chases Rainbows" expresses an intimate bond between two masculine characters who set out on an imperialist enterprise of exploring the Chinese continent while using the all-dialogue form of a film scenario. Same-sex intimacy is linked to national sentiment through the medium of cinema. Albeit, this intimacy is thwarted or unfulfilled in "One Who Chases Rainbows," as one speaker confesses to the other that he does not know his heart.

In the preface to *Small Lyrical Songs* (抒情小曲集, *Jojō shōkyokushū*), put out by Murō and Hagiwara's Sentiment Poetry Company (感情詩社, Kanjō shi sha) in 1918, Murō described the homoerotic nature of his and Hagiwara's friendship, suggesting same-sex desire was part of the atmosphere in which the two men produced their creative output during the three-year period of the journal:

> We boys [私たち少年ら, *watashi-tachi shōnen-ra*] felt for each other a deep love like for a girl, and for the object of our free verse and haiku, we always chose these friends. Beautiful boy companions— at one time, we would talk about poetry, we would warmly clasp hands and kiss, we would take walks during which it was unthinkable to tire of the blue twilight.

> 私たち少年らは、おたがひに女の子のやうな深い情愛をかんじ合つて、かく詩や俳句の対象はいつもそれらの友に於て選んだ。美しい少年の友だちらは、ある時は、詩のことを話したりして、熱い握手や接吻をしたり、蒼い日暮の飽くことをしらない散歩をしたりしてゐた。[48]

In this passage, Murō portrays himself and Hagiwara as part of a milieu of *shōnen-ai* (少年愛), or love between beautiful boys. Jeffrey Angles describes this milieu in Taishō-period Japan as: "a new generation of authors whose writing describes amorous schoolboy relationships based on an appreciation of *bishōnen* beauty and shared interests."[49]

In the book *Love Poetry Collection* (愛の詩集, *Ai no shishū*, 1918), published by the Sentiment Poetry Company, Murō includes a poem addressed to Hagiwara, titled "A Poem For Hagiwara" (萩原に与へたる詩, "Hagiwara ni ataetaru shi"), in which he uses cinematically tinged visual terms to describe his love for the other poet:

> I enter into your breast
> Projected beautifully there
> Now I will never be apart from you.

> 君の胸間にしみ込んで
> よく映つて行つてゐる
> 私はもはや君と離れることはないであらう[50]

The word Murō uses for "projected" (映つて行つてゐる, *utsutte-itteiru*) contains the same character found in the word "cinema" (映画, *eiga*).

Murō thus portrays the two poets' love as a visual image projected on the screen of each other's breasts, redolent of the cinematic works they enjoyed together.

In the years before they founded the journal *Sentiment*, the two men developed a craze for European crime films, including *Zigomar*, *Tigris*, and *Protea*, all directed by Jasset. All three films were released in Asakusa movie theaters. In 1915 in an article in the newspaper *Jōmō Shinbun*, Hagiwara described the two poets' love for crime cinema in the following terms:

> A film with a villain as well as a detective for a protagonist, how superior it was to other entertainments, for this was what drew our interest. The villain Tigris from the *T Gang* as well as the biography of the beautiful woman detective Protea (Asakusa Denkikan[51]) moved the poet Murō Saisei to madness.
>
> Oh how crime itself even has already within it a kind of spirituality. For, oh how to commit violence is at that moment to be able to be the bravest individualist and sentimentalist [感傷主義者, *kanshōshugi-sha*]. Not only that, but he is able to directly encounter the truth, to pull off the mask of hypocrisy and ostentation from the true face of humanity straight on.

> 探偵及び兇賊を主人公とした活動寫眞が他の如何なる演藝にも優つて我々の感興を牽く所似が此處にある。『T組』の兇賊チグリス及び美人探偵プロテヤ（浅草電氣館）の一代記は詩人室生犀星をして狂氣する迄に感激せしめた。
>
> 如何なる犯罪でも犯罪はそれ自身に於て既に靈性を有して居る。何となれば兇行を果せるものは其の刹那に於て最も勇敢なる個人主義者となり感傷主義者となり得るからだ。のみならず彼は直接眞理と面接することが出來る、人類の僞善と虛飾と假面を眞向から引ぱかすことが出來る。[52]

In this quote, Hagiwara characterizes Murō's passion for film as "madness," something that he as the writer of the essay shares. He links crime cinema to a poetics of truth and confrontation, where crime reveals "the true face of humanity." Criminals have a strong sense of self and passionate sense of emotion that makes them the perfect role models for poets like Hagiwara and Murō, who themselves as a kind of passionate brotherhood of poetic crime, bound together as true "individualists and sentimentalists."

In letters from this period, Hagiwara sometimes signs his name Protea, adopting as a nickname the name of the beautiful woman spy from the 1913 film of the same name. Protea, as suggested by her name, is characterized by her talent for change and transformation, a master of disguise who crosses gender lines in her ability to adopt different personas. The beautiful female spy Protea was also an object of fascination for the cross-dressing hero of famed detective fiction writer Edogawa Rampo's (江戸川乱歩, 1894–1965) 1925 short story "Stalker in the Attic" (屋根裏の散歩者, "Yaneura no sanposha").[53] Hagiwara's nickname Protea was thus associated with nonnormative sexuality, crime, and dubious morality practiced by those on the margins of society.

In *Sentiment*, Murō published a poem that can be read in conversation with *Howling at the Moon*'s "Murder Case" and "One Who Chases Rainbows." "Right" (右, "Migi," 1916) imagines a brotherhood of crime, bonded together by intimacy and desire:

Right
Steal,
Steal with your right hand
What only you are allowed to steal,
Which is a spirituality.
The suspect wears a black mask,
We extend our hands to each other,
The evening tears pour quietly over them.
Night is true black of black.
Follow the way of natural rhythm.
Ah, put out the light by the window,
And our comrade wears the black mask.

右
盗めよ
右の手をもて盗めよ
君にのみ盗むことの
一つなる靈性のゆるさる。
曲者はふくめんの黒
手をのべあひて
しづかにそそぐ夕のなみだ。
同志は靈性
夜はしんの黒の黒
しぜんに起るリズムの道を行け。
ああ窓のともしびを消し
同志は黒のふくめんす。[54]

Here, Murō envisions a communion of comrades in black masks, bound by a mission of crime on the margins of society. The thieves are united in an intimate, loving way: "steal/What only you are allowed to steal," so that crime creates a close, conspiratorial connection between the speaker and the second-person addressee. In dialogue with the "lonely" suspect and detective of Hagiwara's "Murder Case," "Right" emphasizes the comradeship of crime, the manly togetherness of its speaker and addressee. While the detective and suspect of Hagiwara's poem are forever alone, in Murō's poem the criminals enjoy a close, intimate connection, thickness amongst thieves. The "spirituality" of their connection recalls Hagiwara's comments in his essay on crime cinema on the spirituality of crime, its capacity to reveal the "true face of humanity." In the "black of black" of night, the comrades are safely concealed, as opposed to the dangerously exposed detective in his glass garment, able to be their true selves in secret spiritual communion.

In dialogue with the two speakers of "One Who Chases Rainbows," it is tempting to read the couple's criminal endeavor as a nationalistic one. Like the two speakers of "One Who Chases Rainbows," the speaker and addressee of "Right" are engaged in a mysterious mission whose ends are unknown. Both couples address each other as *kimi* (君), you, an act of intimacy in the Japanese language, in which pronouns are not grammatically necessary. Both couples are bound by "loyalty," perhaps to the mad emperor of "One Who Chases Rainbows," or perhaps to each other. The thieves of "Right" and the imperialistic explorers of "One Who Chases Rainbows" seem to be two sides of the same coin, homoerotic adventurers whose exploits are narrated by the poet. The adventurers in "One Who Chases Rainbows" are doomed to wander in the open-ended vastness of the Chinese continent, their mission forever deferred and unfulfilled. Perhaps there is a link between Hagiwara's nationalism's tendency to end in failure and foreclosure, and the unfulfilled longing of the same-sex relationships depicted in his poetry. As long as the two men's relationship in "One Who Chases Rainbows" or Murō's "Right" remains unconsummated and deferred, the nationalistic sentiment to which the two men give voice must be stillborn as well. The incomplete, open-ended quality of both notions stands out in high relief when read in the original context of the poetry journal. The poetry of officially licensed state critique gestures to possibilities even as it forecloses them, possibilities of resistance, as well as complicity.

In sum, this chapter has excavated the state critique at work in Hagiwara's writing in *Howling at the Moon* and the early issues of

Sentiment. Through the personal, inward realm of lyric poetry, Hagiwara critiques state efforts to regulate and police human sexuality. In *Howling at the Moon*, especially in the two excised poems and in "Murder Case," Hagiwara writes about nonnormative sex acts in a self-aware way that draws on the constraints of state censorship to make his critique legible as "officially licensed poetry." In *Sentiment*, the intimate "magazine for two" edited by Hagiwara and Murō, the poet critiques the state's imposition of sexual morality while linking sexual desire to the more public political issues of imperial expansion, and even the taboo topic of the emperor's mental health. Together, these writings show how lyric poetry functions as an institutionally licensed space of state critique under the regime of Japanese censorship in the early twentieth century.

CHAPTER 3

"Fragrant Spaces Between Words"
The Oblique Sexuality of Fragrance in Yonezawa Nobuko and Ōte Takuji

"The Expression of Perfume": Scent, Poetry, and Sexuality

We have already seen how Hagiwara Sakutarō uses the poetry of officially licensed state critique to reveal the repressed sexuality in the world of Japanese letters. The poets in this chapter pick up on that thread and use poetry to imagine unrealized possibilities with regard to sexuality and gender. This chapter examines commercial scent, including perfume and incense, in the work of two Japanese poets, Ōte Takuji and Yonezawa Nobuko. In their writings, the sense of smell is associated with oblique expressions of sexual and gender fluidity, including same-sex desire, autoeroticism, and androgyny. They produced these portrayals in a social and literary context of the repression of homosexuality and other socially unacceptable sexual and gendered practices as backward and immoral in favor of modern heterosexuality. The erotic sensuality of their poetry provides evidence that they invested lyric poetry with corporeality and sexuality, arguing for poetry as an act of bodily creation in complex, dynamic relation to social norms around sex and the body.

In her poetry, Yonezawa uses fragrance to obliquely portray the inherent sexuality of poetic creation, creating a feminine, sexual creative voice in a realm, poetry, more often restricted to men. Yonezawa uses the idealized homosocial relationships found in *shōjo* (少女), or girls', culture to imagine a world determined by the creativity and community of women. The relationships between women feature ecstatic sensory pleasure and shared poetic inspiration, brokered by the sense of smell. In this chapter, the sense of smell reveals socially unsanctioned realms of experience.

Yonezawa, born Watanabe Nobuko (Yonezawa is her married name), is a marginal, little-known poet whose work is now beginning to be rediscovered. She self-published one poetry collection during her lifetime, *Holy Fount* (聖水盤, *Seisuiban*), in 1919, and a posthumous collection, which came out in 1937. The themes of femininity, womanhood, and girlhood found in her work draw on her real-life experiences and anxieties. Poet and songwriter Momota Sōji (百田宗治, 1893-1955) once wrote that Yonezawa confided in him that, after graduating from an all-girls high school in 1912, she suffered from depression so intense that she believed she would never be able to marry and have children.[1] In 1918, she married Yonezawa Rizō, a dentist, and eventually they had one daughter named Seiko, whose name features the same first character as the title of her mother's poetry collection, *sei* (聖).

Holy Fount is often referred to as the first free-verse collection by a woman in Japanese. The book met with success for a small, independent poetry publication, selling out its print run of 1,000 copies and enjoying a second edition in 1921. Yonezawa continued to publish poems in a variety of small literary journals. Eventually, she would produce a novel called *Poison Flower* (毒花, *Dokubana*) in 1929 before her death from tuberculosis at thirty-six years old. The novel was awarded a literary prize in the newspaper *Jiji Shinbun* by a panel of Japanese literary giants including Shimazaki Tōson (島崎藤村, 1872-1943), Tokuda Shūsei (徳田秋声, 1872-1943), and Kume Masao (久米正雄, 1891-1952). From her youth, Yonezawa trained in both Japanese and Western visual art and produced paintings, drawings, and other pieces throughout her life. Unlike most of the poets in this study, she is a minor figure in the story of Japanese letters. The feminist poet Takahashi Junko included Yonezawa in an anthology of women's poetry in 2005,[2] and more recently, Andrew Campana translated one of her poems for a current international literary magazine.[3] By including her writings alongside the other major figures in this book, I hope to contribute to the resurgence of interest in her work. The poetry of officially licensed state critique includes canonical figures like Hagiwara and Kitahara Hakushū, as well as more marginal ones like Yonezawa and Ōte.

Although better known than Yonezawa, Ōte is also a minor figure compared to the other poets in this book. Aside from his friendship with Kitahara, Hagiwara, and Murō Saisei, which was largely conducted by letter, he enjoyed few connections with the Japanese poetry scene of his time. Murō, Hagiwara, and Ōte are often known as the "three crows of Hakushū" (白秋の三羽鴉), a testament to the strength of their connection and their discipleship under Kitahara.

Ōte was very shy and introverted, and he only published occasional poems in small, coterie journals, such as Kitahara's *Pomelo* and *Earthly Pilgrimages*, or Hagiwara and Murō's *Sentiment*, as well as small illustrated collections he collaborated on with an illustrator. Even these coterie publications came about only with some persuasion from his friends due to Ōte's reclusive personality. *Tanka* poet Ubukata Tatsue writes that, after being shamed by his grandmother for falling in love with a young male guest at his family's inn in the town of Nishikami-Isobe in Gunma Prefecture, Ōte remained single throughout his life and never enjoyed a romantic relationship.[4] He studied literature at Waseda University and completed a thesis on symbolist poetry. He lived his whole adult life in the same lodgings in the neighborhood of Kagurazaka in Tokyo, and after refusing to inherit the family's inn, he supported himself as a copywriter at Lion Cosmetics, where he met commercial illustrator and printmaking artist Henmi Takashi (逸見享, 1895–1944). Together with Henmi, he put out a small series of illustrated poetry collections, including one with the scent-themed title *Unearthly Fragrance* (異香, *Ikyō*, 1917). He was well read in French symbolist poetry, and a volume of his translations was published posthumously in 1941, again with the scent-themed title of *The Fragrance of Foreign Countries* (異国の香, *Ikoku no kō*). Volumes of his poetry, including *Indigo Toad* (藍色の蟇, *Aiiro no hiki*, 1936) and *Bride of a Snake* (蛇の花嫁, *Hebi no hanayome*, 1940), were also published posthumously, with the support of his friends Kitahara and Hagiwara.

In Ōte's work, fragrance obliquely hints at ways in which gender is fluid. His work features androgyny, cross-dressing, and same-sex relationships between men, which, like in Yonezawa's work, is linked to poetic creativity. "You are pistil and stamen endlessly regenerated" (あなたは たえまなく うまれでる 生涯の花しべ *anata wa taema naku umarederu shōgai no hana-shibe*) he says in a love poem, conjuring an androgynous addressee who has the capacity to endlessly transform and regenerate, with both the vaginal qualities of a flower and the phallic ones of the pistil and stamen.[5] In the early twentieth century,

FIGURE 5. Matsuzakaya advertising circular, August 1932, quoted in "Natsuyasumi yūran nikki." Courtesy of the J. Front Retailing Museum

Japanese literature repressed male homosexuality as feudal and immature to portray a world of modernity and heterosexuality.[6] Ōte's work, like Yonezawa's, expresses a vision of a world where sexual fluidity, far from being repressed and marginalized, is celebrated as an inherent part of poetic creativity. For Ōte, who worked as a copywriter for Lion Cosmetics, this desire exists in tandem with commerce. What happens when sexual fluidity is accepted and can be marketed to the masses in commercial writing? What possibilities exist for how we view both poetry and commerce? The poetry of officially licensed state critique hides in plain sight, operating within the same mass media structures it critiques.

Yonezawa appears at least once in the mass media. She is mentioned in a 1932 advertising circular for the Nagoya department store Matsuzakaya, in the blurb next to a heart-shaped picture of two schoolgirls browsing in the book section.

The blurb cites Yonezawa Nobuko's poetry as a popular favorite among fans of teen girls' culture:

> Young ladies at this age are extremely sentimental. Spilling tears of joy on the front covers of the Takabatake Kashō [高畠華宵] kind of stationery, generally perusing *Wakakusa* [若草] and *Reijokai* [令女界, popular *shōjo* magazines from the 1920s and 1930s], leaving Yonezawa Nobuko's poetry collection idle in her handbag, where it lives with the other texts. Ah! Now with a deep sigh, she has taken another poetry book into her hand... Ooh, *sentimentale*!

> 此齢頃のお嬢さんは断然センチです。高畠華宵描くところのレターペーパーの表紙に随喜の涙をこぼし、若草と令女会は兎に角お読みになり手提鞄の中には米澤順子ものする詩集がテキストと同棲遊ばす......アッ！　只今ふかきため息もて次の詩集を手にとられました．．...．おゝサンチマンタール。[7]

Written a few years after her death, this quote suggests her work might have been taken up by *shōjo* culture retrospectively. Yonezawa's appearance in the mass media reveals how important her poetry was to young girls, and how it served as a treasure alongside other artifacts of *shōjo* culture. The subversive side of her poetry coexists with this almost wholesome, sentimental aspect, embedded in the girl readers' everyday lives. The poetry of officially licensed state critique renders visible the political situatedness of young women like the ones described in the commercial circular, so that the sentimental lament of the girls becomes multivalent and complex.

Interestingly, Ōte, too, has been linked to girls' culture by the poet Shinkawa Kazue, who comments:

> In my house, where there was no interest in the arts, there was no way we would have *Indigo Toad* or *Bride of a Snake*, so it was probably in the kind of supplement often included with girls' magazines, some lovely little poetry collection with a red cover [that I first encountered Ōte Takuji's work]. His verses are filled with the pure emotion of young love, such as the poem "The Little Bird that Nests in the Wind" [風の中に巣をくふ小鳥] that begins "When I first saw you, I became like a gentle wind," or the poem "Dreams that Bloom on the Branches of Sadness" [悲しみの枝に咲く夢] that begins "Beloved, beloved, your breath

gave me sapphire earrings." Even if it were only those two poems, that would be more than enough to attract sensitive young girls. Henceforth, the impression left by the poet Ōte Takuji, of "someone's bashful, gentle older brother," was branded onto my heart, and he was there to stay for a long time.[8]

Shinkawa's evocative account of reading Ōte as a young girl suggests that, like Yonezawa in the department store blurb, Ōte had a presence in girls' culture, and that neither poet shied away from the unabashed emotion and sentimentality often associated with it. Shinkawa remarks that even in a house with little interest in the arts, Ōte's work might have been read because of its association with girls' culture, suggesting that he is a poet whose work is at home in the mass media as it is in the highbrow world of coterie magazines.

Ōte's mass media appearances are very thought-provoking. He wrote the following passage in a June 1931 essay called "On 'The Expression of Perfume:' Idle Chatter" (「香水の表情」に就いて：漫談的無駄話, "'Kōsui no hyōjō' ni tsuite: Mandanteki-na muda-banashi") first published in a commercial periodical called *Tokyo Sundries and Cosmetics Commercial Report* (東京小間物化粧品商報).

> So, for us as amateurs to distinguish "the expression of perfume," the darkness is good; a place where absolutely no noise is audible is good; the morning is good; early summer is good; it is good to be alone; it is good not to speak; it is good to try one perfume per hour; it is good to wait a while after eating; application to a piece of cloth is better than direct use; it is good to experiment twice, with eyes open and closed; it is good to experiment with many different distances; it is good for men and women to experiment separately; a day with no wind is good; and even better is to experiment with the senses in total nudity.

> だから吾々は素人として「香水の表現」を見分けるには、闇のなかがよい、騒音の絶対聞こえない所がよい、朝がよい、初夏がよい、一人で居るのがよい、無言がよい、一時に一つの香水を試みるのがよい、食後相当時間を経てからがよい、直接よりきれ布にでもつけるのがよい、眼をとぢてと眼をあいてと二様に試みるのが良い、距離もいろいろ試みるのがよい、男女別々に試みるのがよい、風のない日がよい、全裸体で感受して試みれば更によい。[9]

Why do Ōte's instructions for how to appreciate perfume involve separation by gender? Why do they involve nudity? The passage obliquely critiques compulsory heterosexuality as promulgated by the Japanese state, and it imagines a world where alternatives become possible.

Fragrance and the Critique of Modernity

Mary Fleischer argues that "smell is the Symbolist sense par excellence . . . used to dissolve barriers between subject and object, between individual and environment."[10] For both avant-garde poetry and the cosmetics industry, the sense of smell plays a key role in imagining and subverting the relationship of bodies to the world and to each other. For Walter Benjamin, Marcel Proust's famous passage on the power of a madeleine pastry's taste and smell to trigger involuntary memory suggests a dialectics or a politics of smell. In Benjamin, the sense of smell brings back alternate temporalities and subverts the inevitability of modernity. Since smell is resistant to capitalist modernity, attempts to commercialize it would of course be really profitable and rewarding: The sense of smell resists easy commodification, hence its value both as a luxury good and as an avant-garde device.[11]

Julia Kristeva acknowledges the vulnerability avant-garde poetry's radicalism to cooptation by commerce. She asks at the end of *Revolution in Poetic Language*:

> Is it possible to keep open the heterogeneous and contradictory moment, which is unbearable for the subject, within a text that represents, through this moment, the diversity and multiplicity of social practices which disregard that moment in their own realization?"[12]

The poems in this chapter tread the line between poetry and commerce. They blur the border between high art objects and commodity goods, keeping open "the heterogeneous and contradictory moment" of their composition and the "diversity and multiplicity of social practices" in which they are embedded.

These social practices included a particular awareness and experience of the sense of smell. As we saw in the passage from his commercially published essay, Ōte uses perfume to elicit a sensory experience of the dissolution of the self and to awaken socially unsanctioned same-sex desires. Ōte's practice exists in what Brian Moeran calls the "olfactory culture" in Taishō-period Japan. In this culture, incense, perfume, and other commercially available scents were enjoyed as a leisure product by ordinary people.[13] They were both diffused in interior spaces for decorative purposes, as well as worn on the body and clothing (mostly perfume, but incense too). From his letters and from the essay quoted earlier, it appears that Ōte composed poetry while enjoying these leisure products, using perfume and incense as inspiration.

The sense of smell thus played a dual role, as an agent of sensory disorientation and the dissolution of the self in experimental poetry, and as a key element of rhetoric in commercial writing in the cosmetics industry. Interestingly, these two roles are not really in conflict with each other. Instead, poets and fashion writers use the sense of smell in parallel, overlapping ways, as we have already seen in Ōte's essay on perfume.

Both poets and fashion writers linked the sense of smell to a critique of modernity and a search for alternative worlds. Beauty and fashion writer Misu Yutaka had the following to say in 1912, the first year of the Taishō era, in a pamphlet on making your own perfume from natural materials like flowers, in which he linked the use of scented products to a critique of "civilization" (文明, *bunmei*):

> Either contemporary people's natural sense of smell is utterly numbed, or is this simply what we call civilization—?
>
> It is said that civilization as such is to be distant from nature[.] Then it is something to be grateful for that most of today's scented products are filled with civilized articles, of course even with the effect that many are expensive. The scented products we smell today—in a word, they don't smell of anything particular at all whatsoever, and thus they do not make one think of anything from nature. Instead, they stimulate people's sense of smell, disorient their spirits, so much so that their excessiveness leads people's lives into error. Therefore, amongst perfumes made with this kind of scented ingredients, and even amongst other cosmetics, it goes without saying that in many cases, the unnaturalness of their scent just toys with and suppresses people's sense of smell.

其れとも現代人の嗅神は自然を嗅ぐべく余りに強く麻痺せしめられて了つたので有らうか、或はこれが文明といふので有らうか―。

自然と遠ざかるといふことは或意味に於ける文明といふもので有らう[。]若しそうとすれば、今日の香料は、殆んど文明的作品を以て満されて居るといひ得ることを感謝する、勿論値段が高いといふことが多きな原因を為しても居やうが、今日我々の嗅ぐ香料といふものは匂い一即ち何物かの匂いこそすれ、其れに依つて自然の何物をも感想せしめざるのみならず、反て人の臭神を刺激し、人の精神を醒亂し、其甚しきに至つては人の命を誤るものすらあるほどで有る、従て是等の香料に依つて作られたる香水は謂ふに及ばず、其他の化粧品に至るまで、其香気の不自然にして只徒に人の嗅神を壓するもののみ多いので有る。[14]

For Misu, smell is a sense that connects people to nature, while civilization (a common Meiji-era buzzword denoting modernity and progress) distances them from nature. Yet this is not to set up a simplistic binary between natural and unnatural: The author is "grateful" for artificial scents that remove one from nature to a certain extent. It is only when they get excessive that he objects, saying they disorient and stimulate people's senses, rather than bringing them closer to nature. Misu's writing suggests an ambivalence towards civilization itself, which has numbed and attenuated people's natural sense of smell. The kind of sensory sensitivity found in Yonezawa's and Ōte's poetry, where smell opens the way to new psychic experiences and modes of being, is perhaps endangered. In dialogue with Misu's remarks, Yonezawa and Ōte's work gestures to a poetics of smell, in which people's natural sensory sensitivity is progressively numbed by the ceaseless advances of civilized modernity.

"Night and Fragrance": Olfactory Culture and Poetic Creation

The olfactory culture of Taishō Japan bridged both avant-garde writing and commerce, which shared the desire for alternative worlds as posited by the sense of smell. Like Ōte, Yonezawa too might have used incense and other scented products to help her compose poetry.

In her poem "Night and Fragrance" (夜と薫香, "Yoru to kunkō"), she describes a first-person speaker's experience of reclining half-asleep and half-awake in a kind of trance on a Western-style sofa for an entire night as she enjoys the smell of aloewood-scented incense. The smell brings her deeply into her body, where she feels her own blood in her heart, and ultimately produces in her a creative act of song. This song, however, is silent (音もなく, *oto mo naku*), a song of bodily experience rather than linguistic, oral, or audio expression. The poem describes the "olfactory culture" of Taishō Japan as practiced by this particular poet, in which solitary bodily experience of scent gives rise to an act of poetic creativity.

Night and Fragrance
Every night
Crossing the pale blue glass door,
With no sound,
Something comes to me in a corner of my sofa
It shines, and yet,
It is talkative, and yet—

From the mouth of the deep bronze urn,
Aloewood's scent profoundly rises,
Everything suppressed in silence,
Colors subdued,
All breathe a secretive sigh.

My heart grows pale,
And dyes itself
The color of dawn, like blood.
Shining thing ever more talkative,
Loudly
Sings laughingly a small song.

夜と薫香
夜ごと
うす青き玻璃戸を越えて、
音もなく、
わがソファの片隅に来るものあり。
輝けども、
饒舌なれどもー

深き紫銅の甕の口より、
浅香の気おもおもと立ち、

ものみな静かに壓さるれば、
色沈みて
かくれたる吐息をなす。

わが心ややに蒼ざめ、
血に似たる
ほどろを染め出せば、
輝けるものいよよ饒舌に、
声高く
おどけたる小唄をうたふ。 15

The first stanza sets the scene in a Westernized Taishō interior, complete with a glass door and sofa. In this setting, the incense appears to be part of the Taishō leisure market, rather than part of any classical Japanese practices around scent. At the end of the stanza, the poem's language splits apart, ending in a dash. While classical Japanese poetry often features fragmented language, the use of punctuation marks the poem as modern free verse. In Heian olfactory culture, which this poem's elegant, mysterious atmosphere recalls, scent had encoded meanings that were canonically recognized in court poetry. In modern times, however, scent is instead a disruptive force, one that puts pressure on language's ability to signify. Notably, there is no reference to an absent lover, a common theme in court poetry. Instead, the speaker appears to burn the incense for its own sake, for sensory pleasure.

The incense is described in terms that suggest secrecy or even illicitness: It is "secretive," "profound," and "suppressed." This creates the impression that the speaker is burning the incense alone, for herself, and that the physical pleasure she experiences is private and personal, rather than embedded in courtly romance and aesthetics. One of the questions with which Yonezawa concerns herself is the social role of poetry: In Taishō Japan, it is a solitary leisure pursuit alongside scent products; while in premodern Japan, poetry was embedded more cohesively in a set of social practices.

The poem ends with the speaker waking up to the reddening of night into daytime, which reminds her of blood. Until this moment, the incense has produced a trance-like state, almost like a drug, and she awakes to heightened sense of her own corporeality as a physical being, with a heart and blood.

The blood creates corporeality, and it also introduces disturbing associations. Is it blood from violence? From sexual experience and the loss of virginity? From menstruation or birth? The end of the night produces an intense sense of the speaker's self as a body, a thing made of blood. The poem ends in song and laughter, a reference to poetry itself as song. The speaker has produced a composition from her body, writing through her experience of fragrance. By submitting to the scent and becoming just a body, she has produced the silent, wordless song of bodily creation. There is an imaginative, speculative tenor to the poem, which imagines a world where the body is not an object of shame or stigma, but rather celebrated for its creative potential.

Perfume, Autoeroticism, and Voyeurism

The oblique eroticism in Yonezawa's poetry becomes more clearly legible in dialogue with some of Ōte's erotic works. For example, in Ōte's 1924 prose poem "Perfume Night Story," perfume is linked to both autoeroticism and voyeurism. The poem describes a nude woman standing in front of a mirror experimenting with perfume, in much the same way Ōte suggests in his commercial essay on perfume quoted earlier. The woman in the poem is in control of her own sexuality, using the perfume to have a powerful sensory experience of her own body.

Perfume Night Story
Inside a dark room, a woman was standing alone.
The room is faintly warm, as if a thin mist pervaded it, murky and yet weightless, as if something's breath was ebbing and flowing, under that soft weight everything becomes totally quiet.
The woman is completely naked. She has not a single piece of cloth on her skin. Not a single ornament on her body.
Her hair is down, just as it is. No oil or comb in it.
On her face, hands, legs, and on her entire body, there is no hint of anything to give her color.
The woman, alive, just as she is, the way she was born. Darkness is sucked into the pores in her skin. The tongue of darkness drunkenly licks her scarlet nails. On her plump, soft thighs, whirlpools of disheveled darkness flow in slow motion.
The woman's pure white body smiles like a warm, large flower. Her hands smile too. Her toes smile too. The woman's rounded body, as if wrapped in white cloud, in the deep purple darkness, ever so slightly, swims smoothly, giving a faint sigh.

The woman is a white owl. Her legs are white swallows.
The darkness goes deeper and deeper into her, sinks into the depths, and emits a faint shadow, while the woman's red lips bite down on tremors of pleasure until they are white, pale.
The woman's eyes grew darker, a faint red like a morning snake, and a bat flees.
The woman is twisted out of shape like a leech, expands, and finally fills the room. Panting, panting, to the point that she's out of breath, close to death.
At this moment, a single droplet of lilac perfume trickles on her left breast. The smell of perfume clings to her breasts, which are small like sakura buds, and vocalizes.

香水夜話

まつくらな部屋のなかにひとりの女がたつてゐた。
部屋はほのあたたかく、うすい霧でもただよつてゐるやうで、もやもやとして、いかにもかろく、しかも何物かの息かがさしひきするやうに、やはらかなおもみにしづまりかへつてゐる。
をんなは、すはだかである。ひとつのきれも肌にはつけてゐない。ひとつの装飾品も身につけてはゐない。
髪はときながしたままである。油もくしもつけてはゐない。
顔にも手にも足にも、からだのすべてに何ひとつとして色づけるもののかげもないのである。
女は、いきたまま、まつたく生地のままの姿である。肌の毛あなには闇がすひこまれてゐる。べにいろの爪には闇の舌がべろべろとさはつてゐる。ふくよかなももには、しどけない闇のうづまきがゆるくながれてゐる。
まつしろい女のからだは、あつたかい大きな花のやうにわらつてゐる。手もわらつてゐる。足の指もわらつてゐる。しろくけぶるやうな女のまるいからだは、むらさきのやみのなかに、うごくともなくさやさやとおよいで、かすかな吐息をはいてゐる。
女は白いふくろふだ。その足はしろいつばめだ。
闇は、きり、きり、きり、きりと底へしづみ、女の赤いくちびるは、白く、あをじろく、こころよいふるへをかみしめて、ほそい影をはいてゐる。
女の眼は、朝の蛇のやうにうす赤く黒ずんできて、いつぴきの蝙蝠がにげだした。

女は水蛭のやうによぢれて、はては部屋いつぱいにのびひろ
がらうとしてゐる。
あへぎ、あへぎ、息がたえだえにならうとしてゐる。
このとき、女の左の乳房にリラの花の香水を一滴たらす。香
水のにほひは、さくらのつぼみのやうなぽつちりとした乳
房にくひついて、こゑをあげてゐる。[16]

Like the solitary speaker of Yonezawa's "Night and Fragrance," the woman in this poem uses perfume to enjoy her own body for herself. She does not instrumentalize her body either for another's pleasure or for socially sanctioned ends like reproductive heterosexual sex. Instead, she enjoys her body for pure sensory experience. The woman applies the perfume at the end of the poem, providing a kind of climax to her pleasure. The perfume "vocalizes" (こゑをあげてゐる, *koe o ageteiru*), allowing her to express herself through her moans, or perhaps through the voice of poetic song.

While the woman seems to be enjoying a purely solitary moment, there are hints of a voyeuristic presence observing her. At one point, the language of the poem shifts from the more neutral である, "*de aru*," to the spoken だ, "*da*," sentence ending, changing from a neutral narrative voice to a tangible, speaking presence observing the action.

What is the relationship between this observer and the woman in the poem? The speaker observes the "voice" to which the perfume gives utterance, but they do not relay the content. The speaker describes admiringly the woman's outer appearance and physical actions, but they do not describe her inner thoughts or her subjectivity.

Yet, by noting the mysterious vocalization at the end of the poem, the speaker indicates that the woman has inner, subjective thoughts of her own, to which she gives voice, even if they are not reported in the poem. As feminist poet-scholar Rachel Blau DePlessis says, "Silence can be the condition of speech unrecorded but alluded to . . . Silence is probably more often a version of the other social situations."[17] Such socially charged silence can portray "[t]he issue of acknowledging speaking others inside the enunciation."[18] While the woman does not directly assert her subjectivity in the poem, that does not mean it does not exist at all. The "unrecorded but alluded to" voice of the woman exists obliquely "inside the enunciation" of the poem, so that the woman character's subjectivity is unveiled while still being oblique.

By placing Yonezawa's poetry in dialogue with Ōte's erotic poem, we can uncover the agency of the female character portrayed there, as well as make more visible the erotic undertones of Yonezawa's work, which echoes Ōte's in so many ways. What would the woman say if the smell that "vocalizes" at the end of the poem could verbalize? In Yonezawa's poems, we have a possible answer.

Birth, Creation, and Poetry as Writing of the Body

In another poem "Hidden Dream" (潜める夢, "Hisomeru yume"), the smell of cinnamon emitted by a Catholic-esque "holy fount" (聖水盤, *seisuiban*) provokes an ecstatic spiritual vision. The end of the poem links this spiritual ecstasy of the holy fount to creating poetry with the body:

> A dream,
> In the shadow of the faintly dark holy fount,
> Submerges its white body,
> Forever giving birth to pure red "creation,"
> Forever singing gold-colored "eternity."

> 夢は、
> ほの暗き聖水盤のかたかげに、
> しろじろと身を潜めつつ、
> 常に真紅の『創造』を生み、
> 常に金色の『永劫』を唄ふ。[19]

The act of creation is coded red, similar to the blood in the vision of the speaker at dawn in "Night and Fragrance." The dream is made corporeal, so that it has a body to submerge in the fount. The submergence of the dream body gives birth to the red of creation, and to a transcendent poetic song of eternity. In sum, the smell of cinnamon inspires a bodily creative act, of giving birth to a poetic song.

What does it mean to give birth to a song, and what does this mean about Yonezawa's view of female sexuality? In the poem "Creation" (創造, "Sōzō") both romantic love and birth are invoked, but in the service of a creative pursuit, rather than coupling or creating a family. She invokes the sense of smell to perform the dissolution of the self and inspire the act of bodily creation.

> **Creation**
> It approaches inquisitively, peering in, formless bondage
> Smoothly

On oh so pliant flesh
Ah
Pleasure the color of flower petals

Pearling drops of oil
Fill my body with an exquisite smell
All of a sudden to love heaven and earth,
Ah,
My heart, may it give birth to a something sublime.

創造
うかがひ寄る無形の緊縛、
なめらかに、
いとも平らけきししむらに
ああ
花びら色の快感。

眞珠なす油のしたたり、
我身常なき香に充ち、
そぞろ天地を戀ふ、
ああ
尊きものを生むこころ。[20]

The poem describes writing as an act of bodily creation, in which the speaker gives her "pliant flesh" (平らけきししむら, *tairakeki shishimura*) over to the "formless bondage" (無形の緊縛, *mukei no kinbaku*) of sensory pleasure, probably a floral-scented oil. The phrase "formless bondage" links the oblique violence of poetic creation with sexual pleasure, so that there is an experience of gaining power through being dominated, of a creative act emerging out of an experience of submission. Throughout Yonezawa's work, the bodily act of creation is framed as passive and submissive, whether an act of "submerging the body" (身を潜め, *mi o hisome*) in "Hidden Dream," or of "formless bondage" in "Night and Fragrance."

Throughout the poem, female sexuality is invoked in oblique terms. While the speaker is not overtly gendered, flowers are often associated with femininity and are a common ingredient in perfume, especially for women's products. The flower's appearance in the poem has kind of a sensual, even a masturbatory quality, how it appears at the moment of pleasure. The masturbatory pleasure of the flower is a creative act, leading to the birth of a poetic song, rather than a child.

The poem features an emphatically physical image of the speaker's body. The "[p]earling drops of oil" that fill the speaker's body "with an exquisite smell" suggest the speaker is using scented oil, but they could also be drops of something bodily, like sweat or discharge. The speaker's body itself is a productive agent, creating drops of liquid and smells that mix with the odor of scented products to provide the speaker with inspiration.

"October Veranda": Female Homosocial Bonding and the Poetics of Scent

In the next Yonezawa poem I will look at, "October Veranda" (十月の凉廊, "Jūgatsu no veranda"), the dissolution of the self is not solitary, but shared by a speaker and a feminine companion. Here the avant-garde pursuit of sensory disorientation through smell is linked to the idealized same-sex relationships between girls often found in popular *shōjo* literature of the day.

> **October Veranda**
>
> Ripe, swaying fennel's faintly sweet
> Cool blue of peppermint left on the round table of the veranda,
> We, cheerfully bathing in October sunlight,
> Somehow even so, we think of undefinable emptiness,
> With forgetful hearts.
> Occasionally, stray locks fall on your forehead.
> You comb them up in the fragrance-filled spaces between words
> —A black comb—
>
> This,
> Is your habit, which reminds me of a young queen.
> Here we are, two women
> Looking up at the October sun.
>
> This gentle breeze filled with zest,
> Softly approaching the marble round table
> Bringing the transparent blue scent of peppermint
>
> Mixing with our voices, lingering with unseen ripples,
> October air filled with dreams
> Layers itself around us.
>
> At a moment like this,
> The round pillar of the veranda, so good for leaning upon,
> —Ah, its mysterious feel to the skin.

十月の涼廊
熟して搖るる茴香のほのあまき、
涼廊(ヴェランダ)の圓卓に置かれたるペパアミントのすずしき青色、
われら、ほがらかに十月の日光に浴しつつ、
なほ、何としもなき空虚を思ふ、
物わすれせしこころ。
ともすれば額にかかる後れ毛を、
匂みちたる言の葉の合間合間にかきあぐる
　-黒き小櫛-

そは、
ふと若き女王を想はする君が癖なり。
ここに女ふたり、
十月の太陽をあふぎてあり。

味ふかき微風(そよかぜ)
大理石(なめいし)の圓卓に忍び寄れば、
ペパアミントの透(す)きとほれる青きかをり

われらが肉聲に混(ま)じりて、見えざる波紋を漂はせ、
夢をふくめる十月の大気、
いよよ身のまはりに重りゆく。

かかるとき、
凭るによき涼廊(ヴェランダ)の圓ばしら、
-あな、奇しきその肌ざはり。²¹

The aesthetics of *shōjo* culture permeate the setting of the poem. It is mysterious and exotic, a Westernesque veranda (written with the Chinese compound *ryōrō* [涼廊], which is sometimes used for the Italian word "*loggia*") furnished with a rounded marble table and pillars that all suggest something like a European villa. The pair of women (ここに女ふたり, *koko ni onna futari*) occupying the space resemble the pairs of graceful women portrayed by popular *shōjo* visual artists like Takabatake Kashō or Takehisa Yumeji (竹久夢二, 1884-1934).

The two women have a passionate connection and appreciation for each other's beauty. Deborah Shamoon argues that *shōjo* culture practices a liminal femininity outside the strictures of marriage and patriarchy—in a safe space that does not actually challenge them. She describes how S relationships are same-sex idealized romantic love that is pure and spiritual, not physical.[22] Together, the two women indulge the sense of smell, as they share an experience of blurring between self and environment. Borders between their bodies and the setting blur due to the intensity of sensory experience. The scene of *shōjo* love includes an eroticized portrayal of language and writing. The words themselves—言の葉, *koto no ha*—are plant-like, emphasizing the "leaf" kanji and filled with fragrance, like the fennel and mint. Perhaps Yonezawa is referring to Yosano Akiko's famous *tanka* collection *Tangled Hair* (みだれ髪, *Midaregami*, 1901), in which tangled hair serves as a figure for both erotic pleasure and the act of writing. Here too the hair is associated with words, and like language with a pen, it can be shaped and formed with the comb. The typography, including several end dashes, draws attention to the materiality of language and its capacity to create sensory experience independent of its communicatory function. Writing, the act of self-beautification or adornment, smell, and a same-sex passionate relationship, are all linked, in a space of the unsaid, between the words.

Shamoon describes how *shōjo* femininity is often misread by Western critics as transgressive because of same-sex romance, when in fact the reality is much more complicated.[23] It would probably be a mistake to read this as a lesbian or queer poem in the usual Western theoretical sense, but there still might be transgression going on in a different way. The radicalism of poetic language, which dissolves borders between self and other and unhinges language from meaning, is not usually associated with the populist realm of teen girl *shōjo* romance. What are the possibilities of this combination? Is the dissolution of the subject through sensory experience really a radical act, or rather a way to sell perfume, incense, and other goods? Maybe, however, it situates the subversion obliquely, in what Yonezawa calls "the fragrant spaces between words" where the body is both present and disavowed. Maybe there are traces of the body once the fragrance dissipates, and these traces are what is not assimilable by commerce.

Smell, Sexuality, Flesh, and the Open-Ended Body

To further bring out the corporeality of Yonezawa's work, I would like to look at the sense of smell in another poem by Ōte. For both poets, the sense of smell operates as an agent of sexuality and the body, often in nonnormative, fluid forms, such as androgyny, sadomasochism, and autoeroticism.

What are the possibilities for this sense of eroticism, neither commercial nor avant-garde, but with elements of both? The 1915 early poem "Flesh Pervades" (ひろがる肉体, "Hirogaru nikutai") by Ōte sexualizes the sense of smell and links it to a sense of androgynous fluidity that exists in ambiguous relation to socially accepted categories.

Flesh Pervades
My voice carries far, like a conch shell horn.
I press down on my stomach and walk forcefully,
Sunbeams scatter away like little red rags,
Air boils up into foam like the breath of pale uterine wall.
Mountains, rivers, hills, and fields, all become one beastly creature, and it follows me.
My feet become soil and spread out,
My body becomes scent and pervades.
Various laws become my feed, as if they were scraps of meat.
In this way, I hide inside the silent conch shell horn.
Deaf moon, blind moon,
I have not yet been extinguished completely.

ひろがる肉体
わたしのこゑはほら貝のやうにとほくひろがる。
わたしはじぶんの腹をおさへてどしどしとあるくと、
日光は緋のきれのやうにとびちり、
空気はあをい胎壁の息のやうに泡をわきたたせる。
山や河や丘や野や、すべてひとつのけものとなつてわたしに
　つきしたがふ。
わたしの足は土となつてひろがり、
わたしのからだは香となつてひろがる。
いろいろの法規は屑肉のやうにわたしのゑさとなる。
かくして、わたしはだんまりのほら貝のうちにかくれる。
つんぼの月、めくらの月、
わたしはまだ滅しつくさなかつた。[24]

This poem was one of the comparatively few that saw daylight during Ōte's lifetime. It was printed in Kitahara's journal *Earthly Pilgrimages* in January of 1915 under Ōte's real name. It was one of the first he published under his birthname, rather than a pen name he adopted early in his life, Yoshikawa Sōichirō (吉川惣一郎). In *Earthly Pilgrimages*, the poem was included in a cluster of works by young poets under Kitahara's mentorship, including Ōte's fellow "three crows," his friends and supporters Hagiwara and Murō.

The speaker of the poem is an androgynous, possibly nonhuman creature whose body has the power to pervade the world around him. The speaker's body experiences constant transformation. By the time readers get to the seventh line, the speaker's body becomes pure smell and spreads out into space (香となつてひろがる, *nioi to natte hirogaru*).

The creature has an outlaw, antisocial quality: It eats laws like scraps of meat. However, it also has a hidden, repressed tendency to hide in its silent shell that counters its bold ability to eat laws, or perhaps enables it to go about its business in secret.

Ōte echoes his portrayal of an open-ended body in an illustration he created in May of 1920. The image was included in his posthumous volume *Bride of a Snake* in 1940.

The drawing depicts an androgynous body whose flesh spreads out in an open-ended manner across the white space of the page, like the "flesh that pervades" of the poem. Below the body, in a star-like formation, it appears there are roots in the earth, or perhaps cosmic limbs stretching out in the sky. The handwritten caption reads "Apparition in Broad Daylight" (白晝の魔物, "*Hakuchū no mamono*"). The term "broad daylight" (白晝, *hakuchū*) suggests a kind of exposure, so that the creature appears openly in public. For shy, introverted Ōte, it feels like a moment of boldness, even defiance, in which the private is made public, the unveiling of an open secret of sorts. Alongside "Flesh Pervades," one of the first poems published under his real name, it feels like a moment of exposure and openness for the famously reclusive poet.

Something that resembles Ōte's "flesh that pervades" appears in the cover illustration of Yonezawa's 1919 poetry collection, *Holy Fount*, featuring a self-portrait by the poet.

In this image, she is singular, not in a pair like what was often seen in images associated with *shōjo* culture. Her hair looks modern, maybe permed, cut short. There is something kind of adult about her, how she is holding her hand with the bracelet. She has a self-possession, a

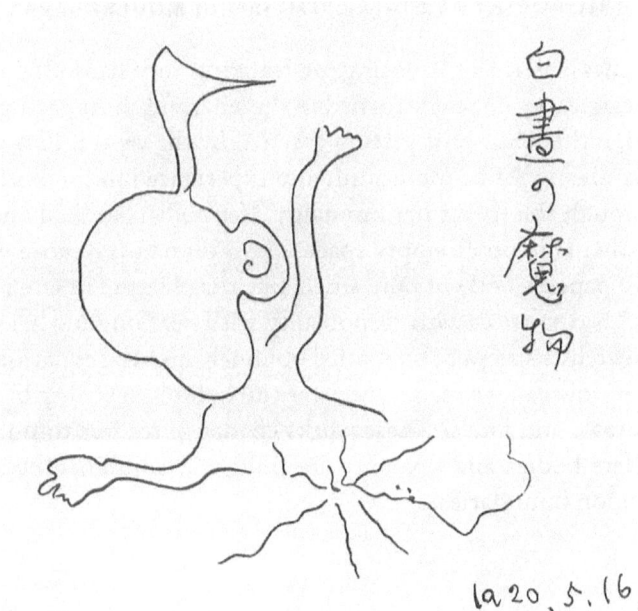

FIGURE 6. Ōte Takuji, illustration, "Apparition in Broad Daylight," May 16, 1920, included in Ubukata, *Metorazaru shijin*, 135.

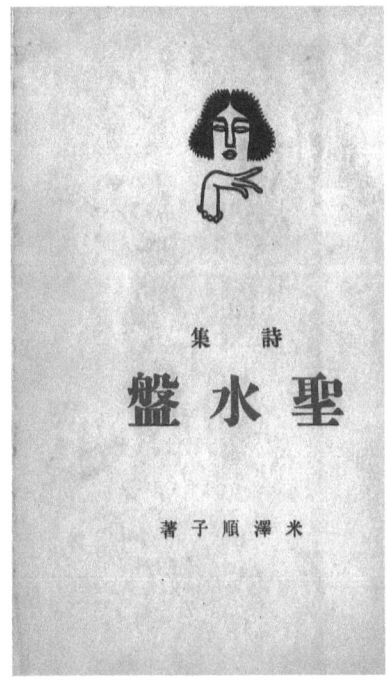

FIGURE 7. Yonezawa Nobuko, cover image, *Seisuiban*, 1919, https://m.media-amazon.com/images/I/410BOHxQcjL.jpg.

deliberateness, as if she is posing, or thinking very hard. She is positioned straight-on, not coyly turned to the side, and she is gazing out of the paper, rather than only getting gazed at by the viewer. This woman seems like she might be more adult and experienced in the world than a *shōjo*, though she shares her liminality. Her body is liminal and ethereal, mostly made up of empty space, like a human fragrance wafting across the paper, a body of pure smell, like the creature in Ōte's "Flesh Pervades." Is this a *shōjo* with corporeality, with her body and her sexuality not entirely disavowed, but added obliquely into the equation using language? How can we readers register the oblique sexuality of poems like Yonezawa and Ōte's? These works challenge readers to imagine a world where bodies and sexuality are fluid, not contained by already decided-upon boundaries.

CHAPTER 4

Ice Land and *Black Cypress*
Lyric Poetry and Photography in a Time of Total War

The Conservative Retreat in Modern Japanese Poetry in *Ice Land* and *Black Cypress*

In a much-discussed conservative turn, starting in 1931 following the Manchurian Incident, many Japanese poets shifted away from the experimental qualities of their early work and toward collaboration with an increasingly repressive state apparatus. Ironically, it was their lyricism, with its focus on the personal, that allowed them to continue to publish in these straitened circumstances, and even to find a newly receptive space for themselves in mass culture, including radio, recordings, and photography, which all found propagandistic uses for poetry as the war continued. Poets took refuge in the personal, romantic realm of lyric poetry and wrote with ambivalent self-consciousness about the genre's incorporation into popular culture in a time of war.

By broadcasting their ambivalent poetic texts in the highly policed idiom of popular culture, these poets reveal the form's ability to work in the oblique register of the "alibi" that André Lefèvre suggests translation (in this case, not between languages, but between media) can provide.[1] How does lyric poetry operate in the popular sphere in a time of war, especially if we accept Theodor Adorno's famous assertion that lyric is "always the expression of a social antagonism" that works by undoing or unsaying itself, enacting its own extinguishment into deathly silence?[2] With what echoes of oblique resistance does this voice of self-silencing resound when it utters itself in the public sphere? Anne-Lise François suggests that it is in this act of unsaying that the political potential of lyric poetry lies, in its ability to speak in the idiom of open secrets, which, in unveiling, unsay themselves.[3]

This chapter will explore the late works of two different poets responding to the unveiling of what was once an open secret in earlier decades before the onset of total war following the Manchurian Incident: war as a fact of daily life in late 1930s Tokyo. The experimental pioneer of free verse Hagiwara Sakutarō, who, as we have seen, in 1917 was the first person to publish an entire poetry collection in vernacular Japanese, responded to the war with a kind of retreat from the experimentalism of his early and midcareer poetry. In the last years of his career, he advocated a "Return to Japan" in a 1937 essay of that title, which was later adopted as a nationalistic call for a uniquely Japanese identity by the Japan Romantic School. The last years of Hagiwara's career are sometimes described as a "shameful defeat" in which the poet reneged on the experimental innovations of his early life.[4] Recent scholars like Tsuboi Hideto and Toshiko Ellis, however, have found that there is more to Hagiwara's late work than this retreat from his early experimentalism, and that his late style is complicated and ambivalent. This chapter seeks to contribute to this resurgence of interest in Hagiwara's late work. Rather than a shameful defeat from his youthful experimentalism, his late work represents a continuation with his lifelong preoccupation with the poetry of officially licensed state critique, especially in its troubled relation to the realm of mass media.

Kitahara Hakushū, whose early work was discussed in chapter 1, experienced a productive flourishing during the war, writing more than ever and enjoying a high degree of popular success in newspapers, records, and radio. While highly successful at the time, Kitahara's wartime output has often been ignored by subsequent postwar scholars who see it as nationalist and propagandistic. Recent scholarship, however, has rediscovered the relevance of Kitahara's late works. Nakano Toshio writes how Kitahara's wartime work was actually continuous with his earlier writing, suggesting that his patriotic songs produced after the Great Kantō Earthquake of 1923 prefigure the ones he produced during the Pacific War.[5] In addition to the continuity that Nakano describes, Tsuboi shows how Kitahara's work on childhood in *Memories* prefigures his involvement with the emerging genre of children's songs or poetry (童謡, *dōyō*), most notably with the journal *Red Bird* (赤い鳥,

Akai Tori, 1918-36), which used children's songs to mobilize children as national subjects.[6] Nakano, Tsuboi, and other recent scholars call on readers to view Kitahara's wartime works in continuity with his earlier work, not as a rupture or aberration.

Hagiwara and Kitahara took two very different paths when it came to their wartime involvement. Kitahara's flourishing output meant he was positioned as a "national poet" (国民詩人, *kokumin shijin*) who worked as a face of the Japanese nationalistic imperial enterprise alongside such nationalistic lyric poets as Miyoshi Tatsuji (三好達治, 1900-1964) and Takamura Kōtarō (高村光太郎, 1883-1956), while Hagiwara was a far more ambivalent figure.[7] Tsuboi suggests that the difference between the two poets comes down to their attitudes toward Japanese as a national language (国語, *kokugo*): Kitahara wholeheartedly embraced it, while Hagiwara was much more ambivalent, if not critical.[8]

Engagement with these poets' wartime works through the lens of officially licensed state critique reveals the complicated nature of collaborative poetry: It is not the wholly enthusiastic embrace of militarism as which it is so often dismissed, but neither does that make it critical of war in the usual antiwar sense. Instead, Hagiwara and Kitahara's war poetry reveals the arbitrariness of the distinction often drawn between jingoistic, collaborative poets who embraced the war effort out of genuine enthusiasm, and virtuous poets who gave in to pressures to print prowar poetry only because of coercive pressure from the state.

Crucial to undoing this binary distinction between enthusiastically jingoistic collaborators and virtuous poets yielding reluctantly to state pressure is understanding these poets' place in the mass media in the 1930s. The war brought them many opportunities to appear in major newspapers, on the radio, and on records, all media that were progressively nationalizing as the war continued. Opportunities for this kind of mass exposure were less common in the prewar period, and poets like Hagiwara and Kitahara produced many thoughtful, ambivalent texts on these media, to which they had been granted greater access than before. Though they had certainly appeared in mass media outlets from time to time in earlier years, these opportunities would not have existed to the same extent without the war and its mass media front.[9] These poets' often fraught attitudes towards radio, film, and other media reveal the difficulty they had navigating their new roles as nationalized poets of the masses enlisted, willingly or not, in a wartime media campaign, either as producers of nationalistic war poetry, or of supposedly innocuous works of lyricism that might offer distraction or consolation to audiences.

This chapter will focus on two collections, one by each poet: Hagiwara's *Ice Land* (氷島, *Hyōtō*, 1934) and Kitahara's *Black Cypress* (黒檜, *Kurohi*, 1940).[10] Both collections are understudied in comparison to the two poets' earlier works. As works produced toward the end of the artists' lives, both *Ice Land* and *Black Cypress* partake of what Adorno and Edward Said referred to as "late style." Adorno's 1937 essay on late style suggests that the formally fragmented quality of works produced at the end of artists' lives represents a response to the ravages of history: "The late works ... show more traces of history than of growth."[11] Adorno suggests that late works' resistance to their own formal unity reflects the damage wrought by modernity upon the artist's subjectivity. Said uses Adorno's term "late style" to describe the "untimely" quality of works produced at the end of artists' lives, by which he means their resistance to the linear timeline of ordinary human life.[12] Both *Ice Land* and *Black Cypress* contain the untimely, ravaged qualities that Said and Adorno say characterize late style. While their authors took very different paths when it comes to the question of their wartime involvement, they share a preoccupation with this notion of lateness. Both poets have faced criticism or lack of interest in their late works because of their turn away from their earlier poetics.[13] Margaret Benton Fukasawa refers to the war poems in Kitahara's *Black Cyprus* as "patriotic" and suggests that they "have lost their relevance for modern readers."[14] Makoto Ueda characterizes Hagiwara's *Ice Land* as "sentimentalist" and a retreat from the "transcendental sphere" of his earlier work.[15] I seek to contribute to more recent scholarship referred to earlier that sees Hagiwara's late works as complex and highly important.

Ice Land was Hagiwara's final collection containing original work. He would produce two more later books that contained reprints of previous poetry. *Ice Land* begins with a prose preface and a haiku by the author setting the scene of the collection in the season of winter. The collection is structured around this central imagery system of winter, ice, and snow. The book is short, with only twenty-five poems in total (not counting the haiku epigraph). Four of the poems are reprints from a series called "Poems of a Distantly Viewed Homeland" (郷土望影詩, "Kyōdo bōei shi"), originally published in a 1925 issue of a poetry journal called *Japanese Poets* (日本詩人, *Nihon shijin,* 1921–26), of which Hagiwara briefly served as editor. Hagiwara adds a series of short prose explanatory notes to the end of *Ice Land*, in which he indicates that he included the reprints because he believed they fit with the rest of the collection. It is probable that Hagiwara also added these poems because they were written in classical Japanese, prefiguring his retreat away from the colloquial. Unlike *Black Cypress*, *Ice Land* contains no war poetry.

Black Cypress was Kitahara's tenth, and second-to-last, *tanka* collection. In it, he comes to terms with his impending mortality and especially the loss of his sight. Fukasawa points out that "[w]ords pertaining to sight appeared in almost every poem," and blindness and vision are its central motifs.[16] He would publish one more tanka collection, one collection of free verse, and a volume of patriotic children's poetry before his death in 1942. There were also unfinished manuscripts, including a collection of free verse poems about his hometown, Yanagawa, accompanied with photographs by collaborator Tanaka Zentoku (田中善徳, 1903-63). *Black Cypress* is quite long compared to *Ice Land*, containing several hundred thirty-one-syllable poems. It is divided into two sections, with the first section comprising about four fifths of the book, and the second section much shorter at about a fifth of the book. The first section contains poems of daily life chronicling the poet's illness and impending blindness. The second section contains largely patriotic military poems. As we shall see in the close readings that follow, the two sections, one about blindness and the other about war, produce a certain tension because of the juxtaposition of the two motifs. It is almost as if Kitahara is making a connection between blindness and warfare. For example, in one poem from the second section, the poet connects the onset of his lost vision to the war in China:

> Ever since the time
> gun echoes roared
> in north China,
> my view has turned dark,
> I have stayed shut in[17]

> Kita shina ni
> hō todorokishi
> koro yori zo
> ma mi kuraku narite
> ware wa komoritsu

北支那に砲とどろきし頃よりぞ目見闇くなりて我は籠りつ

While Kitahara's prowar involvement is undeniable, this *tanka* suggests a dimension of commentary or self-awareness, almost as if the poet is lamenting his own status as national poet. The poem adopts self-consciousness of its own complicity in warfare's effect on civilian life in Japan.

In the prose prefaces to *Ice Land* and *Black Cypress*, the authors both use the politely self-deprecating tone that is common to authors' prefaces. However, this tone takes on a particular intensity so that the authors seem to be making diminished claims for the artistic efficacy of their work. Both authors phrase this diminished claim for their work in terms of an unvarnished document of their personal lives. In other words, they lay claim to their writing as unpolished personal documents rather than self-conscious artistic works. This diminished ambition for their work resonates with the politicality of lyric poetry, the idea that a text's political efficacy comes from erasing or undoing its own utterances.

In his preface, Hagiwara phrases this diminished ambition in *Ice Land* using the book's central seasonal imagery of winter and ice:

In all likelihood, rather than a work of art, this is a document of the author's real life, a sincerely written diary of the heart.

The author's past life was a lonely iceberg's life, wandering the north seas of the arctic pole. Seeing that iceberg's isles emit a hallucinatory aura, the author wandered emptily with the current, by turns troubled, happy, sad, or angry with himself. The author is an "Eternal Wanderer" with no home where he ought to dwell. Above the author's heart, there is always the lonely, clouded sky of the arctic pole, and the wind of the ice land cries out, cutting the soul through. The author has written all these poems as a diary of that real everyday life [實生活, *jisseikatsu*], of that painful living [痛ましい人生, *itamashii jinsei*].

おそらく藝術品であるよりも、著者の實生活の記録であり、切實に書かれた心の日記であるのだらう。
　著者の過去の生活は、北海の極地を漂ひ流れる、侘しい氷山の生活だつた。その氷山の嶋嶋から幻像(まぼろし)のやうなオーロラを見て、著者はあこがれ、悩み、悦び、悲しみ、且つ自ら怒りつつ、空しく潮流のままに漂泊して來た。著者は「永遠の漂泊者」であり、何所に宿るべき家郷も持たない。著者の心の上には、常に極地の侘しい曇天があり、魂を切り裂く氷島の風が鳴り叫んで居る。さうした痛ましい人生と、その實生活の日記とを、著者はすべて此等の詩篇に書いたのである。[18]

Hagiwara's claim that the poems in *Ice Land* were "a diary of that real everyday life [その實生活の日記, *sono jisseikatsu no nikki*]" is especially startling, given his early work's emphasis on the mediation, artifice, and performativity of lyric poetry. Hagiwara had always positioned his work as an alternative to the dominant school of Japanese literature, naturalism, which defined writing as an unmediated account of the author's real life, especially associated with the genre of the autobiographical I-novel, or *shishōsetsu* (私小説). As we saw in chapter 2, Hagiwara's early work in *Howling at the Moon* modeled itself after the character of Protea, the ever-changing spy of many identities who appeared in the film of the same name. In the preface to *Ice Land*, Hagiwara retreats from his early work's emphasis on artifice and self-conscious artistry, and instead uses the rhetoric of personal authenticity. In so doing, he makes a diminished aesthetic claim for his work, which is a mere "diary" (日記, *nikki*), not poetry.

In the preface to *Black Cypress*, Kitahara similarly positions his writing in relation to its truth, authenticity, or realness, though unlike Hagiwara, he throws doubt on its reliability as a document of the everyday:

> A black cypress's silent fallen buds: Can they be contained, or known?
>
> These two and a half years of dusk, I have lived in these circumstances, and at the very least, I offer this elegant inner life. From the beginning I have struggled with the pain of illness, and I do not intend to win out against it this time; nor do I intend to appeal to the world, trusting in darkness; merely the reverse side of mist's suggestiveness; I have only taken from start to finish the path I prefer, a layer of ordinary reverent harmony. Furtively, or rather, secretly, the volume *Black Cypress* ought to be cared for alongside me, and I publish it fearing that the truth may be misrepresented, however slightly. There is nothing else to say.

> 黒檜の沈静なる、花塵をさまりて或は識るを得べきか。
>
> 薄明二年有半、我がこの境涯に住して、僅かにこの風懐を遺る。もとより病苦と闘つて敢て之に克たむとするにもあらず、幽暗を恃みて亦之を世に愬へむとにもあらず、ただ煙霞余情の裡、平生の和敬ひとへに我と我が好める道に終始したるのみ。
>
> 「黒檜」一巻、秘して寧ろ密かに我といつくしむべく、梓に上して些か我が真実の謬られむことをおそる。他に言ふところなし。[19]

There are several parallels with Hagiwara's preface to *Ice Land*. Both of the prefaces seem concerned with this question of the truthfulness of writing: In Kitahara's case he is ambivalent about the danger his writing might "misrepresent" the truth, while Hagiwara not only admits that his true self is on the page, but frames that as a kind of failure, a retreat from art. Neither preface mentions the war, a significant silence considering the time-period of publication. This silence suggests that the poetry of officially licensed state critique operates in terms of the unsaid.

Unlike Hagiwara, Kitahara produced many works of nationalistically tinged war poetry, ones that are often ignored or dismissed by critics. In a *tanka* from *Black Cypress*, Kitahara portrays the warlike, manful spectacle of a Japanese military parade, but does so while fracturing the canonical syllable count of the *tanka* form, giving rise to a moment of disjunction.

> Warriors
> about to die
> gasping for breath
> how they scream out,
> *For the Emperor,*
> *Banzai!*
>
> Tsuwamono wa
> aegu ima wa mo
> o-takebite
> koe age ni kemu
> tennō heika
> banzai
>
> つはものはあへぐいまはもをたけびてこゑあげにけむ天皇陛下万歳[20]

Kitahara's *tanka* describes the soldiers in heroic, idealistic terms, calling them "warriors" (つはもの, *tsuwamono*), rather than the more neutral "soldiers" (兵隊, *heitai*). The language of idealized, warlike masculinity conjures associations of the war poetry found in the eighth-century imperial anthology the *Manyōshū*, then undergoing a renaissance as wartime poets revisited its ideals of "manly heroism" (ますらお, *masurao*).[21] The poem describes the spectacle of militarism, reveling in the display of manly heroism it brings to viewers, whose pleasure is gestured to using the classical past tense suffix けむ, *kemu*, which implies the presence of a speaker recollecting the past.

The poem's overt pleasure in the display of warlike masculinity is complicated, however, by Kitahara's departure from the standard metrics of the *tanka*, which are usually composed in sequences of five and seven syllables, a pattern of 5-7-5-7-7. This poem contains the usual thirty-one-syllable pattern, but then adds an extra four-syllable unit at the end, the word "banzai" (which counts as four syllables in Japanese). While the addition of a single syllable to the standard *tanka* pattern is a common technique known as "extra character" (字余り, *ji-amari*), the addition of four syllables, almost an entire five-syllable unit, is unusual. It is as though the soldiers' cry ruptures the form of the *tanka* itself, exceeding the bounds of canonical poetic expression.

This moment of rupture certainly serves to enhance the manly pleasures of the scene: the soldiers' orgiastic passion is such that it cannot be contained by conventional literary forms. However, it also suggests that there exists a kind of tension between the tanka form and modern war poetry, that the two cannot coexist without creating moments of disjunction. The end of the poem departs so drastically from conventional *shichi-go-chō* (七五調), or 7-5 syllabic rhythm, that it would complicate efforts to chant or perform it orally. The word "banzai" is meant to be uttered aloud, an oral cry by definition, but its place in the poem makes it a barrier to oral performance. Were this poem performed in a sequence of *tanka*, it would be confusing for a casual listener trying to decipher where one poem ended and the next began, leaving the word banzai to hover in a kind of static-filled gap between poems.

Kitahara's nationalistic poem defamiliarizes the orality of the *tanka* form and raises the question of whether classical poetic forms can survive intact their encounter with the overwhelming pleasures of wartime spectacle. As we shall see in chapter 5, the fact that Kitahara disrupts the poem's ability to be smoothly read aloud is highly suggestive in light of his own frequent participation in 1930s oral culture on records or radio. His insertion of the word banzai outside the traditional syllabic bounds of the *tanka* suggests that these mass media broadcasts of his work have a disjunctive effect, giving rise to moments of static that disorient listeners.

Next, I will analyze the two poets' attitude to photography in wartime Japan, with Hagiwara emphasizing the medium's distancing, detached qualities, and Kitahara its potential to create moments of emotion and empathy. Through cinema, oral culture, and photography, these two poets' late works explore the ambivalent position of lyric poetry, sometimes thought of as elite and hermetic, within mass culture, especially the prevalence of militarist nationalism, of which they are critical but in which they are deeply embedded, aesthetically and emotionally.

From Detachment to Empathy: Poetry on Photography

Where *Black Cypress* brims with passionate feeling, *Ice Land* regularly laments the speakers' numbness and lack of emotion. This dynamic emerges in the two books' treatment of photography, where the blank spaces and the unseen become a vehicle for the expression of the two poets' complex attitudes toward 1930s militarization of the nationalized media as a domestic wartime resource. While Kitahara's poems suggest that photography can be a vehicle for moments of empathy between viewers and the subjects depicted, Hagiwara's emphasize the distant, detached quality of photography. Both Kitahara's poetry of photographic empathy and Hagiwara's of chilly emotional distance bring to the fore the question of the ethics of photography in wartime, asking readers to consider whether it can be a vehicle for compassion, or for indifference, and what the stakes of those affective responses are. In so doing, Kitahara and Hagiwara gesture to how both photography and lyric poetry cannot help being intertwined in the wartime mass media as national idioms of expression.

Hagiwara's comments on his own experiments with photography suggest he saw a complex relationship between photography, emotion, and distance. Starting in the 1910s until the 1930s, he was an amateur practitioner of stereoscopic photography, a mode of photography inspired by three-dimensional nineteenth-century panorama entertainments in which two identical photographs are superimposed in order to create a three-dimensional image. In a 1939 essay for the photography magazine *Asahi Camera* he described three-dimensional photography in the following terms:

> Thus, the autumn grass, or the umbrella, or whatever is in the foreground, presses forward, while the background retires one layer further back, and inside a dream of long duration, it feels silent and motionless.[22]

Inspired by Meiji-era panoramic entertainments, Hagiwara's three-dimensional photographs were meant to play with the dimensions of space, to use proximity and distance to create an emotional response in the viewer. By contrast, Hagiwara suggests that the two-dimensional photography which pervaded wartime print media was flat and emotionless, without the power to elicit such a "dream of long duration."

An example of Hagiwara's stereoscopic photography follows:

FIGURE 8. Maebashi: Motion Picture Theater Street, in *Hagiwara Sakutarō shashin sakuhin*, 68–69. Courtesy of Maebashi Literary Museum, The City of Water, Greenery, and Poetry.

This pair of images, labeled "Maebashi: Motion Picture Theater Street" by subsequent editors, depicts a street in Hagiwara's hometown.[23] Stereoscopic photographs were produced in pairs and viewed as a single three-dimensional image using a device called a stereoscope. These photographs use linear perspective to create a sense of depth that would be quite striking when viewed stereoscopically.[24] The street becomes a three-dimensional space that exists "inside a dream of long duration." The movie theater at the edge of the frame enhances the dreamy atmosphere, hinting at the cinematic adventures and experiences that await the passers-by within.

By comparison with the dreamy, three-dimensional quality of his own photographs, Hagiwara's poem "Fire" represents what the poet saw as the flat, emotionless quality of Shōwa print photography. The poem is about a catastrophic fire in an unidentified urban setting.

Fire
Watching the fire burn red
Like beasts
You say nothing, silent.

Fire flames up beautifully,
Into the quiet sky of the city at evening.
Flames quickly flow and spread,
In an instant, they destroy everything.
Capital, factories, large edifices,
hope, prosperity, wealth and rank, ambition,
In a moment, you burn them all down to nothing.

You, fire,
Why do you, like beasts, say nothing,
Silent?
Sealed in lonely melancholy,
And, in this serene, twilit sky,
you pursue passion to its ultimate end.

火
赤く燃える火を見たり
獣類(けもの)の如く
汝は沈黙して言はざるかな。

夕べの靜かなる都會の空に
炎は美しく燃え出づる
たちまち流れはひろがり行き
瞬時に一切を亡ぼし盡せり。
資産も、工場も、大建築も
希望も、榮譽も、富貴も、野心も
すべての一切を燒き盡せり。

火よ
いかなれば獸類(けもの)の如く
汝は沈默して言はざるかな。
さびしき憂愁に閉されつつ
かくも靜かなる薄暮の空に
汝は熱情を思ひ盡せり。²⁵

The setting is described as a "quiet city at evening," a description that suggests the city is rendered silent by the act of photography, and that it is in its declining evening moments as it nears night and extinction. The line "in an instant, they destroy everything" suggests the temporality of photography in times of war or disaster, which exists to distill a catastrophic event into a single moment (瞬時, *shunji*) of total destruction.

Despite the fact that the scene it describes of a major urban fire would surely be loud and cacophonous, the poem emphasizes its total silence, describing the city repeatedly as "quiet" (静か, *shizuka*). The poem does not mention photography; however, the unreality of the fire, which makes no sound, generates no heat, and produces no human victims, suggests that it is a photographic representation rather than a real fire, perhaps printed in an illustrated magazine, which would have been unlikely to print representations of the human damage of the fire.

The city's silence is mirrored by the poem's speaker and his unspecified addressee: "Watching the fire burn red / like a beast / you say nothing, silent." The speaker and his addressee "are silent" (沈默して, *chinmoku shite*) as they gaze upon the disaster, and in keeping their silence, they seem to have lost an essential aspect of their humanity and become "like beasts" (獸類の如く, *kemono no gotoku*). The use of archaic, flowery poetic language like *nanji* (汝, which could also be translated as "thou") and the cutting word *kana* (かな), which often appears as a conventional emphatic word in classical *haikai*, emphasize the speaker's aesthetic detachment from the scene before him, which he writes about in self-consciously artificial terms. Far from creating empathy, the photographic gaze creates detachment, leading the speaker and his addressee to judge the flames "beautiful" (美しく, *utsukushiku*) and describe them in flowery language, regardless of the suffering they create.

The speaker notes the fire's destruction of the city's capitalistic infrastructure, which consumes "everything all at once" (すべて一切, *subete issai*), once again evoking the singular moment captured by photography and its destructive power:

> Capital, factories, edifices,
> hope, prosperity, wealth and rank, ambition,
> all in an instant burned up.

Ultimately, not only the city's capitalistic resources but also human feelings of "hope" and "ambition" are consumed by the flames, the affective underpinnings of capitalistic growth. Ultimately the flames destroy the speaker and his addressee's ability to feel and emotionally connect with one another: "thus too, in the quiet twilit sky/you pursue passion to its ultimate end," says the speaker, suggesting he and his addressee are remembering an intensity of feeling they can no longer experience. They are reduced to silent beasts as they act as spectators of a photographically captured fire.

By contrast, Kitahara's poems about photography emphasize its ability to elicit empathic connections across time and space. For example, in one poem the speaker experiences a moment of connection with a soldier in a photograph in a magazine. The poem is labeled with a note "Looking at a certain illustrated magazine" (ある画報を見て, *aru gahō o mite*).

> Both eyes
> bandaged in white
> a lone soldier
> I don't know where to look

> Moro no me o
> shiroku ōeru
> hei hitori
> miyaru hō da ni
> omooenakuni

両の眼を白く蔽へる兵ひとり見やる方だにおもほえなくに[26]

With its opening phrase "both eyes" (両の眼, *moro no me*), as well as the verb "looking" (見やる, *miyaru*), the poem foregrounds the act of vision and the way it is mediated by print and photography. Drawn together by the medium of printed journalistic photography, the soldier and the speaker turn their eyes away from one another, connecting with one another by not looking, not seeing. The speaker turns away from the reality of war and prefers a world of not-seeing and not-looking.

Kitahara's poems on photography and the act of looking away draw the attention of the reader to what is unseen, what lies in the blank spaces of the photographs with which wartime consumers of media were inundated. In doing so, they create a space in photography for an empathetic connection between seer and seen, a possibility that Hagiwara treats with skepticism in his poem "Fire." These two divergent interpretations of photography in a time of war suggest how the medium itself, and its intermedia translations into and as lyric poetry, can function as a tool either of detachment or of empathetic connection, either highlighting viewers' painful humanity or revealing their loss of it. Which is more troubling: Kitahara's empathetic shock of realization of the suffering of others, or Hagiwara's empty numbness and inability to feel that very empathy?

Reenvisioning the Narrative of 1930s Failure

The preceding chapter has shown how Japanese poets unveiled the ambivalent position of poetry in a time of war, highlighting the pleasures and possibilities afforded by their new access to mass culture, as well as the self-aware critical distance with which they approached these forms. It is one of the interesting ironies of the 1930s period that, because of the state's appetite for poets willing to lend their voices to the imperial enterprise, modern poetry in Japan achieved a height of popularity that it has seldom enjoyed before or since. Poets whose main readership in the 1910s and 1920s consisted of modernist avant-gardes and leftist coteries found themselves with new access to mass media publications and radio broadcasts.

It is difficult to ascertain the reception of these complex, ambivalent poems. It is most certainly true that their popularity at the time was due in large part to their ability to lend their support to Japanese nationalism, but what if their popularity comes in part from their ambivalence about this very support? It is certainly possible that, as much as readers and listeners enjoyed the nationalistic overtones of the works discussed here, they also gleaned the overtones of critical distance with which these poets approached their own collaboration. The 1930s and 1940s are often posited as a time of failure and retreat for Japanese poetry, but what if modern poetry's newfound popularity actually points, not to a failure, but to a shift in register, a shift from the experimentalism of high modernism, not to conservatism, but to the oblique strategies of lyric poetry? What if, in other words, these poems found their mass audience, not only for their collaborative position, but also for their subtextual overtones of ambivalence and even resistance? Such questions point us readers in the direction of recovering the multivalent possibilities of these wartime poems, so often marginalized as relics of patriotic collaboration, a collaboration they critiqued even as they supported it.

CHAPTER 5

Oral Culture and the Poetry of Officially Licensed State Critique

Poets on the Radio: Kitahara and Hagiwara's Oral Performances

Hagiwara Sakutarō and Kitahara Hakushū's late works, including *Ice Land* and *Black Cypress*, offer a meditation on the role of mass media in a time of war, the chance it offers poets to hide in plain sight. This chapter addresses these poets' appearances in mass media, as well as their poems and prose that discuss them. The presence of imagery drawn from the cinematic *benshi*, from radio and recordings, and from photography invites readers to engage with poetry not just as textual, but as a performative, visual, and audio art. These poets treat mechanized media "not only as theme and content, but also in . . . poetry's structure and relative chronology," so that lyric poetry as a mode of writing is transformed by its encounters with these other media.[1]

In this chapter, first, I will explore Hagiwara and Kitahara's vocal performances on 1930s radio and records, the media most closely aligned with the state and its imperial war efforts. Then I will discuss how Hagiwara framed their relationship to mass media in terms of a response to censorship, comparing themselves to *benshi*, silent film narrators who functioned as the often slyly subversive point person between censors and film audiences.

In their poems featured on the radio and on records, Hagiwara and Kitahara extend their self-conscious critique of themselves as mass poets to the aural media most closely tied to the national war effort, due to the state's close involvement in their day-to-day operations. Japanese radio was heavily nationalized from its inception in the mid-1920s, with the state funding the majority of broadcasting stations and maintaining strict control over their programming.[2] Record companies, while operated by private commerce, were often produced with radio broadcast in mind and were therefore also subject to state controls. Even newsreaders' tone of voice was monitored, and anything departing from careful neutrality could be censored from future broadcasts.[3]

Kitahara and Hagiwara's performances use seemingly insignificant oral features to express their ambivalence toward their place as nationalized poets in the 1930s and their nostalgia for an earlier era of modern poetic expression before the codes of censorship became so rigid. An extra syllable orally added to the printed text, a certain monotonous tone of voice: These subtle cues become a way for these poets to assert their subjectivity even as they are instrumentalized by nationalized oral media. In doing so, they point to lyric poetry's complicity in the war effort, in which they too are implicated as poets and performers.

Hagiwara and Kitahara's oral performances for records and radio posit a nostalgic return to the Meiji period as an implicit expression of ambivalence toward their role as nationalized poets participating in the war effort. They characterize the oral culture of the 1930s as mechanized and unpoetic, and offer the Meiji-era practice of chanting poetry as an alternative to the usual poetry readings found on national airwaves.

What were the stakes of the popularity of reading poetry aloud, and how did the form come to exert so pervasive and dominant role in the wartime Japanese poetic world? The practice of poetry readings originated in the 1920s with the People's Poetry Group (民衆詩派, Minshū Shi-ha), who used it as a way to propagate the burgeoning form of *jiyū kōgo shi* (自由口語詩), or colloquial free verse, which was written in contemporary vernacular Japanese rather than classical.[4]

Building on the use of poetry readings by the People's Poetry Group, 1930s poets expanded the practice of oral performance of poetry. Tsuboi Hideto has described the post-1931 era in Japanese poetry as a "return to the voice" (声への回帰, *koe e no kaiki*), a play on Hagiwara's famous essay "Return to Japan" (日本への回帰, "Nihon e no kaiki").[5] The return to orality among Japanese poets in the 1930s represented a reaction against the emphasis on visuality found in the high modernism that dominated poetic production during the 1920s, including the use of the materiality of typography as a poetic device by Surrealists such as Kitasono Katsue (北園克衛, 1902-78), or the use of visual art in conjunction with text by anarchists such as Hagiwara Kyōjirō (萩原恭次郎, 1899-1938) of the journal *Red and Black* (赤と黒, *Aka to kuro*, 1923-24).

When viewed in context with the highly nationalized and censored medium of 1930s radio, Tsuboi's formulation of a "return to the voice" that parallels the nationalistic "return to Japan" suggests that the new emphasis on orality was closely intertwined with the rightward turn of many Japanese poets during the war. Jonathan Culler writes how the rhythmic musicality of lyric poetry is intrinsic to its engagement with ideology: "The great paradox of lyric, as a ritualistic form with occasional fictional elements, is that while frequently it constitutes a complaint about or resistance to the status quo, its social effectiveness may ultimately depend upon some sort of catchiness or memorability."[6] Kitahara and Hagiwara both use what Culler calls the "catchiness" of lyric poetry as an oral form to engage with the ideological structures of their time, to complain about the status quo even while caught up in its maintenance.

The popularity of broadcasted and recorded performances of poems, as well as the adaptation of many poems into popular songs, facilitated the participation of modern Japanese poetry in the war effort, since so many of these broadcasts and recordings were nationalistically themed.[7] Hagiwara and Kitahara express nostalgia for Meiji-era orality. Both expressed ambivalence about the popularity of the *rōdoku* style of reading poetry aloud, instead using the more archaic term *rōgin* (朗吟), which was coined in the Meiji era, when poetry reading was performed in a more musical manner, almost resembling chanting. Their use of the term *rōgin* for the performance of free verse suggests a kind of nostalgia "for the perceived poetic energy of the innovators of the early Meiji," who tried to incorporate Edo-period poetic rhythms and musicality into their reading style, rather than support for the more modern, conversational style of reading favored by *rōdoku* performances usually broadcast on nationalized radio.[8]

While both Kitahara and Hagiwara referred to their poems when read aloud as *rōgin*, interestingly their performance styles when actually reading them aloud are very different. In a series of recordings made for Columbia Records from 1937 to 1940, Kitahara, when reading either his *tanka* or his free verse, performs them in a musical, chant-like manner that emphasizes their use of 7–5 syllabic rhythm (*shichi-go chō*). Hagiwara, however, reads his free-verse poems, which also contain occasional echoes of *shichi-go chō*, in a repetitive monotone. In the 1930s, most poetry recordings and broadcasts featured professional vocal performers, rather than the poems' author, so these recordings represent an unusual chance to examine these two poets' vocal interpretations of their own works at a time when the issue of orality in poetry was particularly charged.

In Kitahara's 1937 oral reading of a series of free-verse poems called "Fragments" (断章, "Danshō") about his childhood memories of listening to music from his 1911 collection *Memories*, his musical, *rōgin*-like delivery suggests nostalgia for the earlier era of Meiji experimentation. Although the poems he performs are free verse, not *tanka*, he reads them in the rhythmic, musical fashion of *tanka rōgin*, rather than the more colloquial, spoken-word style that characterized most *rōdoku*-style poetry readings.[9] The text of Fragment 22 follows:

> Whither my friend?
> The red of late autumn sunset, gazing alone in solitude,
> The unreal high notes flow of the piano keys as they're touched,
> So yet again, alone, alone, today passes.

> わが友いづこにありや。
> 晩秋の入日の赤さ、さみしらにひとり眺めて、
> 搔いさぐるピアノの鍵の現なき高音のはしり、
> かくてはや、獨身の獨身の今日も過ぎゆく。[10]

The poem's use of Meiji-era coinages such as piano further suggest nostalgia for the Meiji era. The Meiji-era association is disrupted when, at one point, Kitahara departs from the written text and inserts an extra syllable in order to make a line fit the 7–5 syllable rhythm: わが友[は]いづこにありや, "*waga tomo [wa] izuko ni ariya*" (whither my friend?).[11] The insertion, the grammatical particle *wa* (は), marks "my friend" as the topic of the sentence. While *wa* was added to fit the 7–5 rhythm and enhance the poem's musicality, it also has the effect of making the sentence more grammatically correct and closer to the rules of vernacular modern Japanese prose. "My friend" is now introduced as the topic of the sentence, rather than suddenly interjected by the speaker in a moment of feeling so intense that the rules of grammar can be bent.

Rather than the experimental rhythms of earlier poets, the line starts to resemble the vernacular poets of the 1930s radio waves, who seek to reproduce the patterns of standardized modern Japanese. The original 1911 printed version allowed the line to stand with a broken *shichi-go chō* rhythm as well as with nonstandardized syntax, while the 1937 oral reading smoothed over this irregularity.

Kitahara reads with a quality of melancholy and sadness that suggests a dimension of self-awareness or ambivalence about his own act of standardizing or smoothing over the irregularities in the Meiji-era text with the vocal mannerisms of Shōwa mass orality. His vocal performance is quiet and soft, almost fragile, creating a sense of regret and melancholy. The speaker smoothing out his own once-experimental and recalcitrant poems does so while looking back at his youth with longing and regret.

The vocal softness of the performance suggests the lassitude of an aging speaker looking back on childhood and highlights the temporal return at work in Kitahara's oral rendition of his twenty-year-old poem. The piece first appeared in his 1911 collection *Memories*, which was about the poet's childhood in the town of Yanagawa in southern Japan. The text's original place in a sequence of childhood reminiscences suggested that the scene it describes is one of the speaker's loneliness as a child, a "lonely" (さみしら, *samishira*) boy standing by the window and "looking out alone" (ひとり眺めて, *hitori nagamete*), wishing for friends to play with. Kitahara's 1937 performance of the poem, shortly after the publication of a series of *tanka* in the journal *Tama* describing his diagnosis of diabetes, which would soon lead to the loss of his vision, recontextualizes the speaker's loneliness. Now, instead of a young child looking out the window and wishing for playmates, the speaker is an old man losing his vision and contemplating his mortality.

For 1937 Kitahara, the piano underlines the ambivalence with which he vocally edits his early work to make it fit the landscape of Shōwa mass orality, with its emphasis on vernacular Japanese and 7–5 syllabic rhythm. The piano, which was often featured as accompaniment in the *kineorama* shows that Kitahara attended as a youth, suggests associations with the Meiji-era media landscape. Its music, along with the *benshi*'s narration, would have provided the live soundscape for the proto-cinematic entertainments that the childhood speaker might have enjoyed. The nostalgia for the prewar past expressed in the poet's image of the piano tugs at the reader's heart, undoing its own poetic utterance even as it embodies them.

Elsewhere in the original 1911 collection Kitahara is reading from, in the poem "Shadows" (陰影, "In'ei"), which he does not perform in his 1937 poetry reading, the piano appears as an accompaniment, not only for the *kineorama* entertainment, but for memory itself: "Oh *kineorama* of my truly young days, / Piano accompanying from the shadow of my memory" (げにげにわかき日のキネオラマよ、/ 思ひ出はそのかげに伴奏く ピアノ).[12]

This passage from Kitahara's 1911 work casts his 1937 recorded performance in a different light: the piano to which the child speaker listens is part of a Meiji-era live media soundscape. The piano's music summons "memory" (思ひ出, *omoide*) in the "shadow" (かげ, *kage*) of the *kineorama*'s images, providing a kind of shadow memory where the speaker's childhood memories blur with the images cast by the projecting device. In light of the piano's association with the *kineorama*, the child speaker of "Fragments" becomes a consumer of media, as he "touches the keys" and listens to the "unreal high notes" (現なき高音(ね), *utsutsu naki takane*), unreal perhaps because of the fantastic cinematic images they recall, and looks out the window, which resembles a screen because of its large, flat quality and its visual function. As the child wishes for a friend to play with, the piano summons memories of his cinematic shadow self. The longing and ambivalence with which the child grown old summons memories of his Meiji-era cinematic life implicitly critiques the heavily censored media environment in which his oral performance appears.

While Kitahara's oral performance expresses ambivalence toward the mass production of oral poetry by hearkening back to Meiji-period forms of orality, Hagiwara's monotonous, dry reading style emphasizes the mechanical, inhuman quality of 1930s oral culture. In contrast to Kitahara's musical reading, Hagiwara's vocal performance is repetitive and drone-like. Hagiwara was also a shy personality, and it is possible that his flat reading style comes from simple nervousness. Nevertheless, the mechanical quality of Hagiwara's reading style suggests a kind of refusal of Kitahara's nostalgia for Meiji orality, or perhaps an awareness of the impossibility of such a return. It is also notable that while Kitahara reads from an early collection, perhaps the equivalent of a music performer playing their hit songs, Hagiwara reads from his more recent late works rather than his more famous earlier poems.

Hagiwara's reading aloud of "Nogizaka Club" (乃木坂倶楽部, "Nogizaka kurabu"), from *Ice Land*, was recorded in 1940.[13] In the recording, Hagiwara reads each line in the same rhythm and tone, with a downward drop at the end of each line as though at the end of a sentence. While Kitahara read with musicality and smoothness, sometimes without making a pause at the line break, Hagiwara ends each line of the poem with the same downward drop in pitch and a brief pause, even if the line break comes in the middle of a sentence enjambed to the next line. This choppy vocal performance creates a sense of constant interruption rather than smooth, flowing syntax, almost as if the recording is punctuated by static.

Hagiwara's interruptive reading style performatively highlights themes of rupture and disjunction in the poem.

Nogizaka Club
December has come again.
What is this winter cold!
This past year I lived in a fifth-floor apartment
in a desolate Western-style room
sleeping lonely in a bed pushed against the wall.
What am I thinking?
I am tired of life's falsehoods
even now all the more hungry like domesticated animals.
I have not been deprived of anything
yet I have lost everything.
How, as though pursued,
I depressively wandered the busy end-of-year streets
and even in the daytime I get drunk in a seat at the bar.
My emotions too certainly disappear into the distant past.
Like a bird flying away into the empty sky

December has come again.
What is this winter cold!
A visitor knocks at the door,
sees my idleness, pities me, and leaves,
but with no coal, no hearth
in the desolate, white-walled Western-style room
I wake alone on the bed
and sleep in the daytime too like a bear.

乃木坂倶樂部
十二月また来れり。
なんぞこの冬の寒きや。

去年はアパートの五階に住み
荒漠たる洋室の中
壁に寝臺(べっと)を寄せてさびしく眠れり。
わが思惟するものは何ぞや
すでに人生の虛妄に疲れて
今も尚家畜の如く飢ゑたるかな。
我れは何物をも喪失せず
また一切を失ひ盡せり。
いかなれば追はるる如く
歲暮の忙がしき街を憂ひ迷ひて
晝もなほ酒場の椅子に醉はむとするぞ。
虛空を翔け行くの如く
情緒もまた久しき過去に消え去るべし。

十二月また來れり
なんぞこの冬の寒きや。
訪ふものは扉(どあ)を叩(の)つくし
われの懶惰を見て憐れみ去れども
石炭もなく煖爐もなく
白堊の荒漠たる洋室の中
我れひとり寢臺(べっと)に醒めて
白晝(ひる)もなほ熊の如くに眠れるなり。[14]

For example, Hagiwara inserts his usual downward drop in pitch followed by a pause between the following two lines: "I depressively wander the busy end-of-year streets / and even in the daytime I get drunk in a seat at the bar." Hagiwara's voice comes to a stop at the end of the word *mayoite* (迷ひて, wandering), so that the act of wandering becomes a gap or aporia in the poem, a barrier to the continued act of utterance. Wandering represents a gap in the poem's transition to oral text, a gap that opens up the possibility for the poet to express his ambivalence about that transition.

In the prose preface to *Ice Land*, Hagiwara states that he sees these works as primarily oral texts, written in the melodious *rōgin* style of Meiji orality, rather than the colloquial, spoken style of Shōwa *rōdoku*:

[a]ll these poems are "*rōgin*," to be sung with the emotiveness of *rōgin*. The reader should read them aloud and should by no means read them silently. This is "poetry to sing" [*utau tame no uta*

(the character *shi* annotated with the *furigana*, or phonetic reading, "*uta*")].

すべての詩篇は「朗吟」であり、朗吟の情感で歌はれて居る。讀者は聲に出して讀むべきであり、決して默讀すべきではない。これは「歌ふための詩」なのである。[15]

In light of Hagiwara's emphasis on song (*uta*) and musical, chant-like oral reading (*rōgin*), we would expect that his performance on Columbia Records would resemble the musical, flowing style of Kitahara. His language in the preface suggests that he shares Kitahara's nostalgia for Meiji-period orality, which infuses the other poet's rhythmic, musical vocal performance with melancholy and ambivalence. However, the droning, repetitive manner in which Hagiwara reads his poetry suggests that this is far from the case. Rather than performing Kitahara's melancholic return to Meiji orality, Hagiwara's reading highlights the impossibility of such a return by deliberately avoiding expressivity and musicality alike. Hagiwara's songs are difficult, recalcitrant ones that stick in the throat and cannot be sung—and yet, he says in the preface, they must not be read silently either (決して默讀すべきではない, *kesshite mokudoku subeki de wa nai*).

Perhaps Hagiwara's expressionless reading style represents an attempt to give voice to a kind of silence, a song that sings of its own impossibility, the impossibility of producing lyric song in an era where it is broadcast en masse. The lyric song's complicity in the war effort obstructs its ability to sing in the first place. Like the speaker in "Nogizaka Club," who, "like a bear" (熊の如く, *kuma no gotoku*), hibernates the day away "inside the white-walled, desolate Western-style room" (白亞の荒漠たる洋室の中, *haku'a no kōbaku taru yōshitsu no uchi*), it seems that Hagiwara has chosen reclusiveness and silence, rendering himself incapable of human speech, and sealing his poetic voice inside the homogenous, white-walled confines of the Western-style radio broadcast of free verse.

Isoda Kōichi has noted how this poem combines autobiographical fact with performative fictionality. He points out that Hagiwara had recently moved back to Tokyo and lived in an apartment introduced to him by fellow poet Miyoshi Tatsuji, but the poem's description takes several liberties. The room was likely a "high-class apartment" rather than the desolate dwelling portrayed in the poem, and Hagiwara even fictionalizes what floor he lived on (in the poem, he says it was the fifth floor, when, in reality, it was the second).[16] Isoda argues that these fictionalized elements create a desperate, depressive persona that the poet is playing based on elements from his real life.[17]

Hagiwara's vocal performance resonates with Isoda's reading of the poem: at once raw and emotional, as well as highly performative and mediated. As we have seen in Kitahara's melancholy, lamenting oral performances, and in Hagiwara's mechanized, emphatically unemotional ones, these poets brought a degree of self-conscious critique to their encounters with mass media, offering a dimension of commentary on their own acts of collaboration in wartime mass media.

The Poet as *Benshi:* Lyric Poetry's Conservative Turn and Cinema's Transition to Sound

Both Kitahara and Hagiwara attempted to create a lyric voice under the strictures of wartime censorship using idioms and formal devices borrowed from mass culture, which was under severe censorship and scrutiny in the 1930s. In particular, Hagiwara aligned their straitened position with the trajectory of the Japanese film industry, which was undergoing an immense shift in the 1930s as silent films accompanied by live oral narration were replaced by talkies with prerecorded sound, first on records and then as part of the projected film. Yasu Satoshi writes that Hagiwara's work throughout his career was intrinsically related to modernity as a phenomenon of mass media, reading Hagiwara himself as a type of media.[18] My study follows Yasu's lead in situating Hagiwara as a poet of the mass media, alongside Kitahara (though, as I have mentioned in chapter 4, the two approached things in very different ways—Kitahara as a national poet, and Hagiwara as a more ambivalent figure).

Many, particularly those in the Pure Film movement (純映画劇運動, Jun eiga geki undō), advocated for Japanese cinema to shed its Meiji-era theatrical, oral qualities and instead progress toward what they saw as a more modern, purely visual experience of cinema. However, these poets' elegiac evocations of their youthful moviegoing memories expressed ambivalence about the move away from the orality and performativity of Meiji cinema. Most of all, they expressed nostalgia for *benshi*, silent film narrators, who, while responsible for carrying out the censors' edits to their scripts, which were often handed to the narrator directly from a censor attending the screening, also managed to push against the pressures of censorship in small but significant ways.[19] Hagiwara's 1917 formulation of "officially licensed poetry" could perhaps be applied to the *benshi*, too, who operated in tandem with state regulations.

The replacement of *benshi* with recorded sound, as well as the increasing repression that came with 1930s militarization, meant that there was far less room for such ingenious responses to the censors' commands. By looking back to the Meiji period, when *benshi* were considered the first film stars, with loyal followings of fans who came to the theater expressly to see their favorite performers, Hagiwara implies a sense of identification with *benshi* of times past, who were at once censorship's enforcers and its oblique critics.

In the predicament of silent film narrators, who once were able to get away with subverting the censorship rules they were tasked with enforcing, Hagiwara and Kitahara saw an echo of their own difficulties of maintaining lyric expressivity in a time when the ability to express one's individual subjectivity was under pressure from censorship. Beginning in the 1920s, *benshi* were required to support the censors' versions of the films they narrated, rather than obliquely subverting them as sometimes happened in the Meiji and Taishō periods. Film reformers, including the advocates of Pure Film, pressured *benshi* to bring less expressiveness and individuality to their performances and instead to function as explicators of the film, thereby "rendering themselves invisible and supporting the illusion that the text spoke itself."[20] These invisible *benshi* managed to prolong the era of silent film into the 1930s in Japan, by promoting the illusion that their narration was a transparent, unbiased presentation of the film, rather than a performative interpretation of it bolstered by pressure from film reformers and state censorship.

Even then, later *benshi* found ways of asserting their artistic subjectivity, pushing back against pressure to function as transparent explicators of their censor-approved texts.[21] In their wartime works, Kitahara and Hagiwara found ways of "rendering themselves invisible," as Aaron Gerow says of the *benshi* in later years, taking refuge in the oblique and supposedly hermetically personal realm of lyric poetry, evading the censors' commands even as they fulfilled them.

Like the *benshi*, whose role was declining more and more as they were expected to merge with the cinematic text and give up their distinctive voices, the poets in these works attempt to preserve some trace of agency while they lend their voices to the advance of audiovisual technologies and their increasing militarization. In 1942, shortly before his death, Hagiwara remarked on the similarities between free verse (自由詩, *jiyū shi*) poets seeking to reach mass audiences during the war and the now passé craft of the *benshi*:

Once long ago, when silent film was ubiquitous, there were explainers called "*benshi.*" They were in fact a kind of oral poet, adding a high level of intonation and rhythm to their words, making all their explanations into a kind of free-verse-like beautiful style, and how ardently, how sonorously, they delivered their explanations. The explanations of Somei Saburō [染井三郎], Tokugawa Musei [德川夢声], and other such famous *benshi* truly were a kind of beautiful style, and they were at the same time a mode of free verse with its own rhythm. Therefore, it hardly needs saying that their explanation, among young people searching for poetry, had great charms and was welcomed. Even the youth of the masses, with no understanding of poetry at all, were highly compelled by the oral poetry of these motion picture *benshi*, and at one time, imitations of them were fashionable among the youth of the masses.

かつて昔、無聲映畫が普遍して居た時、所謂辯士と稱する説明者が居た。これが實に一種の朗讀詩人であつて、言葉に高い抑揚と節奏をつけ、すべての説明を自由詩風に美文化して、いかにも情感的に、朗々と辯説した。

染井三郎とか、德川夢聲とかいふ當時の名辯士の説明は、それ自體が全く一種の美文であり、且つ一種の節律を持つてる自由詩であつた。したがつて彼等の説明が、詩を求める頃の若い人たちの間に、非常な魅力を以て歡迎されたことは言ふ迄もない。文學の詩に對しては、全く理解を持たないやうな大衆青年でさへが、この活動辯士の朗讀詩にはすつかり魅了されて、當時大衆青年の間に、その模倣が大に流行したことがある。[22]

It is important to note that the essay containing these comments was reprinted in a state-supported anthology of nationalistic war poetry, *A Poetry Collection of Great Japan: To Sing of Holy War* (*Dai Nippon shishu: Sei sen ni utau*, 大日本詩集:聖戰に歌ふ 1942). Therefore, Hagiwara's nostalgia for the "beautiful archaic style" of *benshi* narrators, and its potential to serve as poetry of the masses, was proffered in service to the Japanese war effort. In this passage's nostalgia for the Meiji-period *benshi*, who so cleverly responded to their role as mouthpieces of film censorship, Hagiwara implies an ambivalence towards his own role as a public face of national poetry, including his appearance in the nationalistic collection carrying these remarks.[23] He makes a subtly critical comparison between poets cheering the masses on with their nationalistic poetry (works such as his own "On the Day of the Fall of Nanjing" published five years previously, or Kitahara's 1940 military *tanka*) and *benshi* evading the same morality laws they were tasked with enforcing. Hagiwara and his fellow nationalized poets, his glowing recollection of the *benshi* suggests, could afford to learn a thing or two from their dying art.

This passage on *benshi* narration presents the lost art as a potential first step toward reenvisioning poetry as a popular mode of expression. With nostalgia for the Meiji-period world of cinema viewing, Hagiwara's comments frame *benshi* narration as a retrospective art whose time has passed, repeatedly using such temporal phrases as "once long ago" (かつて昔は, *katsute mukashi wa*). He describes their linguistic style as "beautiful archaic style," or *bibun* (美文), suggesting its self-consciously archaicizing nature. Like the free-verse poets who Hagiwara says they inspired, *benshi* were translators who created a new idiom in modern Japanese, drawing on classical literary and performance forms and on the dialogue of Hollywood and other foreign films. The *benshi* "rhythm" (what Hagiwara refers to as *sessō*, 節奏, or *setsuritsu*, 節律) drew on the 7–5 syllabic rhythms of classical Japanese poetic forms, as well as on modern colloquial Japanese, including both central Tokyo standard and local, especially Osaka, variants.[24] Their textured, rich use of language enabled them to provide unique and sometimes subversive interpretations of the films they narrated, enabling the kind of oblique evasions of censorship that we have seen. For Hagiwara and other poets seeking to make the most of their new popularity on the airwaves and in newsprint, the *benshi* offered a kind of model for hiding in plain sight.[25]

"How ardently, how sonorously, they delivered their explanations," he exclaims, with a kind of lament that the expressivity and lyricism of the *benshi*'s "beautiful archaic style" are no longer current.[26] Hagiwara's comments about the lost art of the *benshi* indicate the qualities which he attempts to ironically resurrect in his own late poems about cinema. For example, he produced a series of prose sketches called "My Favorite Movie Actors" (私の好きな映画俳優, "Watashi no suki na eiga haiyū," 1926), which addresses in turn three major Hollywood silent film stars, Buster Keaton, Charlie Chaplin, and Harold Lloyd. In this poem, Hagiwara portrays his own retreat, his late works' descent into silence, reclusiveness, and reduced artistic expressivity, by aligning this transition in his work with the advent of talkies and the end of silent film and the *benshi*. All three stars had careers that were negatively affected by sound, a transition that was under way in 1926 when Hagiwara published the poem in the small literary journal *Out of Order* (*Fudōchō*, 1925-29), edited by novelist and critic Nakamura Murao (中村武羅夫, 1886-1949). Though the poem contains no explicit mention of the *benshi*, as novelist Haniya Yutaka (埴谷雄高, 1909-97) points out, many of the early Hollywood films were first mediated for Japanese audiences by *benshi*, so the encounter with these actors that Hagiwara describes implies the presence of a *benshi* in the poem.[27]

In addition, the pleasurable intimacy the poem's speaker expresses towards his beloved stars has a subtle homoerotic undertone, thereby obliquely subverting morality laws against depictions of homosexuality. Hagiwara had already experienced brushes with morality censorship for depictions of nonnormative masculine sexuality earlier in his career, for example in 1917 when the poem "The One who Loves Love," which describes a masculine speaker wearing female clothing and makeup while making love to a tree, received a warning for obscenity in his poetry collection *Howling at the Moon*. Hagiwara's fraught negotiations with censorship extended from the political realm to that of morality, and both were intertwined in his poetry on cinema.

The poem's speaker resembles a *benshi* in his ability to adopt different personas and points of view, and in his ability to serve as a model for the sometimes illicit pleasures of the average movie viewer:

Buster Keaton

Always wearing a flimsy hat, with an old-fashioned, slightly tanned face, Buster Keaton! You are a nineteenth-century man of passion, aren't you? And you, an earthy, handsome hick, hold your Western umbrella well.

When European civilization first invented the lamp, you sat beneath it reading a book. I know that book's name. It was printed in woodblocks of old: *A Guide to Physical Science*.

In the 1820s, when those old steam trains seen in lithographs first came to your country town, your elderly parents, carrying an old-fashioned travel bag, looked back at you and said, "Hey Keaton! This is called civilization and enlightenment!"

And so the child, once arrived in Chicago, went to see the Worlds' Fair for the first time, entered inside a mysterious planetarium, and saw a *kineorama* of celestial travel and assorted magic of physical science. And he also saw "Balloon Ride," on the roof of the panorama pavilion, where he gazed at a flag with a mysterious skull on it. That was the eerie sign that spoke of "the mysteries of science."

Keaton! You are not one for modern life. You live alone in nature's forests, longing for far-off civilization as you float your boat in the silent stream, enjoying primeval fishing. Buster Keaton! Just like many comedians, you are one of the "lonely ones."

ばすたー・きーとん

いつも薄べったい帽子をかぶって、古風な浅黒い顔をしている、ばすたー・きーとん！ 君は十九世紀の情熱家だね。さうして西洋雨傘を伊達にさしている、田舎の土くさい色男だ。

欧羅巴の文明開化が、始めて洋燈を発明した時、君はその下で本を読んでた。私はその本の名前を知ってる。それには昔の木彫活字で『理学のしるべ』と書いてあった。

西洋千八百二十年頃、あの銅版画にみる昔の汽車が、初めて君の田舎に来たとき、君の年とった両親たちは、古風な旅行鞄を手にさげながら、君を顧みてかう言った。

「きーとんや！ これが文明開化といふものだ。」

さうして市加古に出て来た子供は、始めて展覧会を見物し、ふしぎな天文館の中に這入って、天界旅行のキネオラマや、理学のさまざまの魔法を見た。或は「風船乗り」を見物し、パノラマ館の家根の上に、奇妙な骸骨の旗を眺めた。それは「科学の不思議」を語る薄気味の悪い記号だった。

きーとん！ 君は近代生活のものでない。君は自然の森林に一人で住み、遠く文明にあこがれながら、静かな流れに船を浮かべて、原始の魚釣りを楽しむんだ。ばすたー・きーとん！ 多くの喜劇役者がさうであるやうに、君もまた生来の「寂しき人」の一人である。[28]

Sometimes he addresses the actor in the second person as *kimi* (君), you, with effusive exclamations like, "Buster Keaton! You are a nineteenth-century man of passion [情熱家, *jōnetsuka*]!"[29] These moments of lyrical address position the poet as a kind of audience surrogate, carried away with fannish enthusiasm for his favorite star as he projects his fantasies about the kind of passionate man he imagines Keaton to be. The speaker addresses Keaton in the second person, an act of intimacy in the Japanese language, where pronouns are often omitted unless inserted for particular emphasis, to the point where second-person pronouns are sometimes translated into English as "dear" or "darling." Sometimes the speaker provides lines of dialogue, not for

Keaton himself, who remains a silent screen on which to project the fantasies of others, but for other characters, such as Keaton's parents, who cheerfully bid him goodbye at the train station as he goes to Chicago, encouraging him to pursue his dream in the big city: "Bye Keaton! This is called civilization and enlightenment [文明開化 bunmeikaika]."[30] Speaking dialogue for the characters positions the speaker as a kind of dutiful, neutral *benshi* who overdubs the dialogue for viewers without comment or interpretation of his own, as befits the role of impartial explicator or *setsumeisha* (説明者) that the *benshi* was expected to play in the late 1920s. The speaker oscillates from infatuated, "passionate" spectator to dutifully relaying the parents' dialogue. However, the overly didactic line "This is called civilization and enlightenment" (これが文明開化といふものだ, *kore ga bunmei kaika to iu mono da*) suggests that the *benshi* takes the parents' dutiful farewell less than seriously.

The line just quoted about "civilization and enlightenment" also expresses the speaker's ambivalence toward modernity. Iijima Kōichi has pointed out that the 1926 poem is concurrent with the start of Hagiwara's retreat away from the experimental modernism of his earlier work.[31] Iijima also suggests that Hagiwara physically resembled Keaton, suggesting that the poem is something of a self-portrait.[32] The speaker as *benshi* uses Keaton to express his lament for the passing of the silent era and a concurrent side of his own poetic enterprise. He depicts Keaton with a tone of nostalgia for what the speaker sees as his optimistic interest in and excitement about science and modernity. The object of the speaker's nostalgia is not the nationalistic premodern past at stake in nationalist poems such as Kitahara's 1940 militarist *tanka*, but rather the potential and excitement of an earlier phase of modernization. As the 1920s drew to a close, Hagiwara's portrayal of Keaton as an optimistic Meiji-era man of sensual pleasures and scientific knowledge implicitly posits this earlier period as a time when the possibilities offered by modernity for new experiences—sexual, aesthetic, and political—were not yet foreclosed.

The portrayal of Keaton as an elegy for the optimism of an earlier era of modernization combines language of progress and advancement with that of nostalgia and remembrance. The poet portrays Keaton as an early adopter of the latest developments in science and technology, who as a child sits under "the first lamp" ever generated by "European progress and civilization" (欧羅巴の文明開化, *Yōroppa no bunmei kaika*) and reads a book titled *Guide to Science* (理学のしるべ, *Rigaku no shirube*).³³

The speaker narrates Buster Keaton's visit to a "wondrous planetarium" (ふしぎな天文館, *fushigi na tenmonkan*) and a *"kineorama* of celestial travel" (天界旅行のキネオラマ, *tenkai ryokō no kineorama*), evoking images of proto-cinematic forms of visual entertainment. Keaton's "wondrous" (ふしぎ, *fushigi*, wondrous, mysterious, uncanny) proto-cinematic visual spectacle contrasts with the dulled, melancholy portrayal of movie theaters and entertainments in *Ice Land*, where Asakusa's famous Luna Park is described as an alienating place where the speaker and a partner ride one of the location's many attractions, an imitation airplane, only to sit in silence, "side by side in contemplation, lonely" (側へに思惟するものは寂しきなり, *kata e ni shi'i suru mono wa sabishiki nari*).³⁴ Keaton's portrait is infused with the speaker's nostalgia for when these new technologies were exciting and full of possibility, before the disillusionment of *Ice Land* has set in.

At the end of the poem, Keaton retreats from the thrills of modernization and finds refuge in a pastoral scene, where he lives "alone in the woods and forests of nature" (自然の森林に一人で住み, *shizen no shinrin ni hitori de sumi*). This retreat seems a place not of refuge and rest, but of loneliness and alienation. The speaker says Keaton "longs for far-off modern civilization" (遠く文明にあこがれ, *tōku bunmei ni akogare*), implying that his remove from these things has left him with some sense of discontent and yearning (あこがれ, *akogare*) for the world of urban modernity that he left behind. Like the reclusive, disillusioned speakers of Hagiwara's wartime collection *Ice Land*, Keaton has lost his taste for the modern sensory pleasures of the city, but he does not seem to take much comfort in his pastoral refuge, either. "You too are one of the naturally lonely ones" (君もまた生来の「寂しき人」の一人である, *kimi mo mata seirai no "sabishiki hito" no hitori de aru*), the speaker tells Keaton in the poem's final line. The speaker's use of the phrase "you too" (君もまた, *kimi mo mata*) seems to offer the lonely recluse some form of hope and undercut the bleak loneliness of the ending. Even if he is alone, the speaker shares his experience of alienation, and some form of communication and bonding between them is possible.

Hagiwara's poem on Keaton foreshadows the reclusive world of his 1930s poems, where the formal experimentalism of his earlier work recedes in favor of performing its own silence. Hagiwara uses the transition of early Shōwa cinema to metaphorically highlight the transition occurring in his own poetic trajectory, away from the excitement and optimism of Meiji- and Taishō-era experimentalism, and toward a retreat into the world of lyricism. Hagiwara's earlier effort, from 1926, compensates for the decline of the *benshi* by allowing the speaker to give voice to different personas and characters. Hagiwara's "Buster Keaton" performs a return to Meiji-period oral practices of cinema, using the obsolescence of the *benshi* to represent the poet's own conservative turn and to point to his use of the alibi of mass culture in the face of intensifying censorship.

In this chapter, I have shown how the uneasy dynamic of self-aware complicity characteristic of the poetry of officially licensed state critique manifests in the vocal performances of the poets themselves and in Hagiwara's "Buster Keaton." Each in his own way, Kitahara and Hagiwara valorize the silences and gaps that emerge in lyric poetry, whether these appear in the elegiac gestures at a lost mode of Meiji orality in Kitahara's case, or in Hagiwara's unemotive performance of the rote quality of the 1930s mechanization of poetry reading. The poem "Buster Keaton" self-consciously laments Hagiwara and his colleagues' turn to reclusiveness and silence in the face of increasing wartime imperialism. It is worth noting that both the vocal performances and "Buster Keaton" posit a return to the Meiji period as a possible balm or escape from the intolerable present moment. This Meiji nostalgia stereoscopically overlaps with the Meiji-period Pan poets' own longing for other worlds—Edo or foreign lands— earlier in the century. Lyric's longing for imagined, unrealized worlds persists during the imperial wartime regime, but is its utopic charge a mode of resistance, or a way to more effectively perform the role of national poet? In the vocal performances, Kitahara's voice is emotional and full of depth of feeling, while Hagiwara's is flat and emotionless. This gap represents the two poets' differing stances with respect to wartime complicity: Kitahara must perform with all the emotionality of the national poet he has become, while Hagiwara can hardly bring himself to participate at all. In dialogue with the poets' vocal performances, "Buster Keaton" suggests a poetics of censorship, wherein Hagiwara occupies the position of officially licensed poet once again, offering an oblique critique of the Japanese state via utopian longing for the world to be different.

Conclusion
"Poetry Gods" and the Legacy of Officially Licensed Poetry

The poems discussed in these chapters relay fragments of feeling from the past with intensity and passion even as they refrain from an explicit political stance. This intensity is positioned in the realm of officially licensed dissent—at once critical of and complicit in the ideological and political structures that underlie it. Like the speaker in Hagiwara Sakutarō's famous poem "Murder Case," the poets in this book are ambiguous, liminal figures: not a criminal, nor an agent of the state, but someone hovering between these two positions. Officially licensed poets seek at once to perpetrate crimes against the state even as they police those very crimes themselves. They submit to what Yonezawa Nobuko calls the "formless bondage"[1] of the law, even as they lament that very bondage. In so doing, they reveal the law's insidiousness, how poets enforce the obscenity laws on their own work using the smokescreen of lyric poetry. These poets approach their collaborative position with self-awareness, so that they operate as national poets even while expressing critical ambivalence about the national enterprises they support. Paradoxically, their ambivalence makes them more effective as purveyors of Japanese nationalism, since readers can relate to their complicated, mixed feelings. These poets lament the "formless bondage" in order better to submit to it, and they submit to it in order better to lament. Hiding in plain sight, they write for readers who lament their own complicity within the proscribed realm of poetry as officially licensed state critique.

In closing, I will show how the poetry of officially state critique persists into the postwar period. In a poem called "Poetry Gods" (詩神, "Shishin," 1973), poet Tamura Ryūichi (田村隆一, 1923-98) offers a possible reading of how some trace of the lyrical prewar past survives in a postlyrical future.[2] Like many members of the postwar Arechi (荒地, "Wasteland") poetry group, of which he was a founding member, Tamura's relationship to the prewar generation of lyric poets remained relentlessly critical, without ever quite reaching a point of decisive break. Most Arechi poets, including Tamura, served as conscripts in the Japanese military during the Pacific War. To Tamura and his colleagues, prewar poets' participation in and support for Japanese imperialist efforts presented a formidable difficulty in any attempt to situate their own poetic work. As the T. S. Eliot reference in their group name suggests, the Arechi poets often looked to European modernists for inspiration, rather than Japanese poets implicated in the war effort that had such devastating effects on their lives. Yet the Arechi poets could not ignore the work of the prewar lyric poets in this book.[3]

In "Poetry Gods," Tamura portrays his intimate yet critical relationship with the prewar generation of poets. The first line of "Poetry Gods" refers to Saitō Mokichi (斎藤茂吉, 1882-1953), a prewar *tanka* poet, while the Asakusa place markers allusively conjure the Tokyo neighborhood where many prewar literary coteries worked and played, near where, for example, Hagiwara and Murō first saw the films of Victorin Jasset.

Poetry Gods

For the god of Mokichi's *poésie*
the Kannon and broiled eel of Asakusa

Because for him there were the ramparts of form
he only went as far as Kaminari Gate

My nervously disposed gods
are always unhappy with something   they don't even have fire insurance

small houses and
great silences

CONCLUSION

詩神
茂吉のPoésieの神さまは
浅草の観音さまと鰻の蒲焼

かれには定型という城壁があったから
雷門へ行きさえすればよかった

ぼくの神経質な神は
いつも不機嫌だ　　火災保険もかけてない

小さな家と
大きな沈黙[4]

The poem comes from Tamura's 1973 poetry collection *New Year Letter* (新年の手紙, *Shinnen no tegami*), named after a 1939 W. H. Auden poem of the same title. One important aspect of Tamura's work is his near obsession with the previous generation of poets, both in the West and in Japan, and his attempts to situate his own work in relation to his predecessors. Auden was committed to poetry as an autonomous entity that, he said in a 1940 elegy to W. B. Yeats, "makes nothing happen," and Tamura was highly drawn to that aspect of Auden's work because so many of his heroes collaborated with the war effort. Saitō, for example, who Tamura cites in "Poetry Gods," produced prowar poetry, instrumentalizing poetry for political, propagandistic ends. Christopher Drake relates how Tamura was deeply affected by the complicity of prewar poets:

> At this time Takamura Kotaro, one of the greatest prewar free verse poets, was writing lines like "Remember December 8 / It cut world history in two!" and the renowned modern tanka poet Saito Mokichi (addressed in Tamura's poem "Gods of Poetry") was writing "When I hear / that war / has started / I hear the roar / of victory itself."[5]

The aftermath of the war and poetry's direct implication in it haunts "Poetry Gods." With a gentle, wry tone, the poem seems to ask how it is possible to read and write poetry after its complicity in the horrors of twentieth-century history, perhaps synchronizing with Theodor Adorno's famous 1949 provocation about poetry after Auschwitz.

Tamura's formal gesture of linked yet discretely fragmentary couplets plays on the same lyrical quality reinvented by the generation of prewar poets he addresses with gentle mockery as his "poetry gods." In Tamura's "Poetry Gods," though the "ramparts of form" that once fortified a previous generation of poets may no longer be available to those writing in their wake, the "small houses" of contemporary verse cannot help but echo their predecessors across the "great silences" of history. The "small houses" also call out to the damaged landscape of postwar Tokyo, the many dwellings lost over years of warfare.

In this poem, Tamura critically approaches the traces of lyric, acknowledging its troubled history without quite foreclosing the possibilities it offers for a postlyrical future. The ghosts of Auden and Saitō hover over the poem, suggesting that poetry's role in history combines the resistant potential of the one with the complicity of the other. Tamura's poem shows how the uneasy positioning of prewar poets like Kitahara Hakushū, Hagiwara, Yonezawa, and Ōte Takuji at once resistant and complicit, remains in the texts' afterlife by calling on the reader as an active participant. The "great silences" Tamura mentions do not have to invite cynical resignation to the way things are, though that tone is undeniably present in the poem. Silence can also contain unrealized possibilities for human beings' social world. The poem's elegiac tone toward the vanished world of prewar Asakusa, the playground of the prewar poets, invites readers to imagine a future social role for poetry, one where it is involved in human community.

Tamura's "Poetry Gods" offers a case study in the poetry of officially licensed state critique that looks back at the past while imagining a tentative future for the lyric enterprise. Self-aware of its own complicity in the structures it critiques, the poetry of officially licensed state critique does not offer transcendence or even resistance. The poet is not a heroic, lone figure standing up to the powers that be, but rather a vehicle for collective yearnings for the world to be otherwise that operates in the shadow of surveillance. Indeed, the poetry of unlicensed dissent relies on state control to make its poetic enterprise work. The poets of the Pan Society (discussed in the introduction) cried out for a more socially connected role for lyric poetry in an alienated world, expressing lyric longing in a utopian register. All the while, the Pan Society (named after the god of song, not bread) remained conscious of the police presence in the room next door, surveilling the poets who critique them. It is this self-conscious awareness of state pressure that gives the poetry of unlicensed dissent its emotional impact. The police presence underlines the impossibility of lyric song, how it sings of the disintegration of the same modern self for which it speaks. The poets of officially licensed critique strain against the constraints of state power and domination, without ever naming them.

Acknowledgments

I first fell in love with modern Japanese poetry thanks to careful and supportive mentorship from Norma Field and Katsumasa Nishihara.

This book began as my PhD dissertation. I'm very thankful for funding from the University of California, Berkeley's Department of East Asian Languages and Cultures and the Center for Japanese Studies, as well as the Japan Society for the Promotion of Science. Many friends helped me get through that time, especially Miyo Inoue, Sumi Lee, Rachel Carden, David Humphrey, Andrew Leong, Lisa Hofmann-Kuroda, and Chelsea Ward. I am also very grateful to my dissertation supervisors Dan O'Neill, Miryam Sas, and the much-missed Lyn Hejinian. I'm also thankful for Toshiko Ellis, an invaluable reader and mentor.

I'm also grateful for funding from the University of Notre Dame's Liu Institute for Asia and Asian Studies and to my colleagues at that institution. At McGill University, many helped with the preparation of this book, especially including Emma Jiarong Wang, Yuriko Furuhata, Gavin Walker, Maria Hwang, and Hye-Jin Juhn. I'm also very grateful for funding from McGill University's Department of East Asian Studies and the Fonds de Recherche du Québec. This book also owes a great deal to the help and mentorship of the late Takako Lento. It is also a great honor to receive funding from the Tanikawa Shuntarō Fund to support translation and scholarship of modern Japanese poetry.

I'm also very grateful for the support of my family, especially my parents Susan and Nathan Tarcov, my brother Gideon Tarcov, my twin Olivia Tarcov, and Bonnard.

Notes

Introduction: The Politics of Lyric and the Poetry of Officially Licensed State Critique

1. Kinoshita Mokutarō, "Pan no kai no kaisō," in *Kinoshita Mokutarō zenshū*, vol. 13, ed. Noda Utarō (Iwanami Shoten, 1982), 157. The term "Japanese-style room" is a little vague and could mean a number of different things, from a modern-style bar to a more old-fashioned establishment to a room in a private home. Kinoshita does not specify beyond "Japanese-style room" (日本室).
2. For example, Merry White, *Coffee Life in Japan* (University of California Press, 2012), 46.
3. Kinoshita, "Pan no kai," 157.
パンの会は、江戸情調的異国情調的憧憬の産物であつたのである。
4. Yoshii Isamu, "Ōkawa Hashi," in *Dai Tōkyō Hanjōki, Shitamachi-hen*, Akutagawa Ryūnosuke, Izumi Kyōka, Kitahara Hakushū, Yoshii Isamu, Kubota Mantarō, Tayama Katai, and Kishida Ryūsei (Kodansha, 2013), 194.
5. Takagai Hiroya, *Hakushū* (Shoshi Yamada, 2008), 169.
6. Kitahara Hakushū, "Sora ni makka na," in *Jashūmon* in *Hakushū zenshū*, vol. 1, ed. Nakajima Kunihiko (Iwanami Shoten, 1984), 29.
7. Nakamura Shin'ichirō, *Waga kokoro no shijin-tachi: Tōson, Hakushū, Sakutarō, Tatsuji* (Ushio, 1998), 136.
8. Theodor Adorno, "On Lyric Poetry and Society," in *Notes to Literature*, vol. 1, ed. Rolf Tiedemann, trans. Shierry Weber Nicholsen (Columbia University Press, 1991), 50.
9. Theodor Adorno, "On Lyric Poetry and Society," 45.
10. David Der-Wei Wang, *The Lyrical in Epic Time: Modern Chinese Intellectuals and Artists Through the 1949 Crisis* (Columbia University Press, 2015), 2.
11. Hagiwara Sakutarō, letter 619 to Maruyama Kaoru, in *Hagiwara Sakutarō zenshū*, vol. 13, ed. Itō Shinkichi, Nakagiri Masao, Naka Tarō, Satō Fusayoshi, Hagiwara Yōko (Chikuma Shobō, 1976), 411.
12. Hagiwara, *Hagiwara Sakutarō zenshū*, vol. 13, 411.
13. Kondō Yōta, "Sensō-shi no jōken," *Gendai Shi Techō* 5 (2001): 45.
14. Tsuboi Hideto, "Kokugo, kokushi, kokumin shijin: Kitahara Hakushū to Hagiwara Sakutarō," *Bungaku* 9, no. 4 (1998): 67.
15. Hagiwara Sakutarō, "Nankin kanraku no hi ni," in *Hagiwara Sakutarō zenshū*, volume 3, 137-138.
16. Hagiwara Sakutarō, "Nankin kanraku no hi ni," *Asahi Shimbun*, December 13, 1937, https://xsearch-asahi-com.proxy3.library.mcgill.ca/.

17. Elise K. Tipton, *Modern Japan: A Social and Political History* (Routledge, 2008), 114.

18. Tipton, *Modern Japan*, 100.

19. Barbara Johnson, "Teaching Deconstructively," in *The Barbara Johnson Reader*, ed. Melissa Feuerstein, Bill Johnson González, Lilli Porten, and Keja L. Valens (Duke University Press, 2014), 347.

20. Jonathan Stalling, *The Poetics of Emptiness: Transformations of Asian Thought in American Poetry* (Fordham University Press, 2011), 12.

21. Peter Fenves, "Benjamin, Studying, China: Toward a Universal 'Universism,'" *positions: asia critique* 26, no. 1 (February 2018): 49. Fenves notes that Benjamin's formulation "utopian images" in his early writings may draw from passages in Wilhelm's translation of Laozi: "At the beginning of "Das Leben der Studenten" ('The Life of Students')—an exoteric essay that complements the esoteric 'Metaphysics of Youth'—Benjamin refers to certain 'utopian images' (GS, 2:75) without naming any. The penultimate chapter of the *Daodejing* can be seen as one of the images to which he refers, for it presents an image of political order on the hither side of all physical despotism. Here are its opening lines, retranslated from Wilhelm's translation: 'May the country be small / And have few people. / Let there be tens or hundreds of devises, / None of which are used. / Let the people take death seriously. / And not roam afar' (Laozi 1910: 85). And here are the final lines, which Benjamin cites at the beginning of the second section of 'Metaphysics of Youth:' 'Neighboring lands may live within visible proximity of each other, such that one can hear on either side the call of roosters and dogs, yet nevertheless the people die at the ripest old age without traveling hither or thither' (GS, 2:96; Laozi 1910: 8)."

22. Christopher Bush, *Ideographic Modernism: China, Writing, Media* (Oxford University Press, 2010), 107.

23. Takayuki Tatsumi, *Full Metal Apache: Transactions Between Cyberpunk Japan and Avant-Pop America* (Duke University Press, 2006), 6.

24. This translation is from *Kokinshū: A Collection of Poems Ancient and Modern*, trans. Laurel Raspel Rodd, with Mary Catherine Henkenius (Cheng and Tsui, 2004), 35. The original is from *Kokinshū*, ed. Kyusojin Hitaku (Kyuko Shoin, 1991).

25. Quoted in Paul S. Atkins, *Teika: The Life and Works of a Medieval Japanese Poet* (University of Hawai'i Press, 2017), 140.

26. Atkins, *Teika*, 140. Atkins further notes that recent research suggests the entry was added retrospectively in 1221, making the *Meigetsuki* "something approaching—but not equaling—memoir, with a retrospective process of editing and redacting during the copying process" (144).

27. Ivo Smits, "The Poet and the Politician: Teika and the Compilation of the Shinchokusenshū," *Monumenta Nipponica* 53, no. 4 (Winter 1998): 428.

28. Scott Mehl, *The Ends of Meter in Modern Japanese Poetry: Translation and Form* (Cornell University Press, 2022), 5.

29. Inoue Tetsujirō, Toyama Masakazu, and Yatabe Ryōkichi, *Shintaishishō*, 1st ed. (Maruyazen, 1882), https://dl.ndl.go.jp/info:ndljp/pid/876377.

30. Maeda Ai, "Utopia of the Prisonhouse: A Reading of *In Darkest Tokyo*," trans. Seiji M. Lippit and James A. Fujii, in *Text and the City: Essays on Japanese Modernity*, ed. James A. Fujii (Duke University Press, 2004), 59.

31. Michael Bourdaghs, *The Dawn that Never Comes: Shimazaki Tōson and Japanese Nationalism* (Columbia University Press, 2003), 6.

32. Miyazaki Koshoshi, Tayama Katai, Matsuoka Kunio, Saganoya Omuro, and Kunikida Doppo, *Jojōshi*, ed. Miyazaki Kokoshi (Tōji Shobō, 1964), 35.

33. Wang, *Lyrical in Epic Time*, 5.

34. James R. Morita, "The *Jojōshi*," *Journal of the Association of Teachers of Japanese* 10, no. 2/3 (September 1975): 184.

1. Critiquing Meiji State Modernization Efforts in Kitahara Hakushū's *Memories*

1. Kawamoto Saburō, *Hakushū bōkei* (Shinshokan, 2012), 92.

2. Kawamoto, *Hakushū bōkei*, 97.

3. Margaret Benton Fukasawa, *Kitahara Hakushū: His Life and Poetry Kitahara Hakushū: His Life and Poetry* (Cornell University Press, 1993), 26–27.

4. Quoted in Kawamoto, *Hakushū bōkei*, 98.

5. Fukasawa, *Kitahara Hakushū*, 30–31.

6. Katsuhara Haruki, "Sakutarō to Hakushū," in *Ishikawa Takuboku to Kitahara Hakushū*, ed. Ueda Hiroshi and Nakajima Kunihiko (Yūseidō Shuppan, 1989), 205.

7. H. D. Harootunian, "Between Politics and Culture: Authority and the Ambiguities of Intellectual Choice in Imperial Japan," in *Japan in Crisis: Essays on Taishō Democracy*, ed. H. D. Harootunian and Bernard Silverman (Princeton University Press, 1974), 123.

8. Harootunian, "Between Politics and Culture," 145.

9. Harootunian, "Between Politics and Culture," 128.

10. Harootunian, "Between Politics and Culture," 128.

11. Vera Mackie and Yamaizumi Susumu, "Introduction," *Japan and the High Treason Incident*, ed. Ben Middleton and Masako Gavin (Routledge, 2013), 4.

12. Evelyn Schulz, "Narratives of Counter-Modernity: Urban Spaces and Mnemonic Sites in the "Tōkyō Hanjōki," *European Journal of East Asian Studies* 2, no. 1 (2003): 148.

13. Kitahara Hakushū, "Ōkawa Fūkei," in *Dai Tōkyō Hanjōki*, vol. 1, *Shitamachi-hen*, Akutagawa Ryūnosuke, Izumi Kyōka, Kitahara Hakushū, Yoshii Isamu, Kubota Mantarō, Tayama Katai, and Kishida Ryūsei

14. See Fukasawa, *Kitahara Hakushū*, 2.

15. *Yanagawa horiwari monogatari*, directed by Takahata Isao (Nibariki/Studio Ghibli, 1987), https://archive.org/details/Yanagawa-Horiwari-Monogatari.

16. Kitahara Hakushū, *Omoide*, in *Hakushū zenshū*, vol. 2, ed. Nakajima Kunihiko (Iwanami Shoten, 1984), 10.

17. Schulz, "Narratives of Counter-Modernity," 149.

18. Kitahara, *Omoide*, in *Hakushū zenshū*, 2: 10. "Ash-colored coffin" is Margaret Benton Fukasawa's translation: Fukasawa, *Kitahara Hakushū*, 7.

19. Fukunaga Takehiko, *Haishi*, in *Fukunaga Takehiko denshi zenshū*, vol. 5, ed. Nishizaka Masaki and Asano Seiji (Shōgakukan eBooks, 2019).

20. Kitahara, "Taiyō," in *Hakushū zenshū*, vol. 2 (Iwanami Shoten, 1984), 198–200.

21. Miki Taku discusses *"nanban shumi"* in Kitahara's early work in Miki Taku, *Kitahara Hakushū* (Chikuma Shobō, 2005), 66–67.

22. Gerow discusses the protocinematic qualities of *gentō* and other visual entertainments (*misemono*) in Aaron Gerow, *Visions of Japanese Modernity: Articulations of Cinema, Nation, and Spectatorship, 1895–1925* (University of California Press, 2010), 41.

23. Gerow, *Visions of Japanese Modernity*, 51.

24. The Liver Taker, a creature that cuts out people's livers in their sleep, appears in folklore. Miki suggests stories of the Liver Taker arose in response to cholera epidemics in the Meiji Period. See Miki, *Kitahara Hakushū*, 11.

25. Kitahara Hakushū, "Yoru," in *Hakushū zenshū*, vol. 2 (Iwanami Shoten, 1984), 200–202.

26. Miki, *Kitahara Hakushū*, 11.

27. Hozumi Akiyuki, "Tozasareta mura de 5 nin no josei o satsugai . . . naizō o eguri totta otoko no 'hontō no nerai,'" *Gendai Bijinesu*, September 26, 2020, https://gendai.ismedia.jp/articles/-/75896.

28. Susan L. Burns, "Constructing the Body: Health and the Nation in Nineteenth-Century Japan," in *Nation Work: Asian Elites and National Identities*, ed. Timothy Brook and André Schmid (University of Michigan, 2000), 27.

29. Fukasawa, *Kitahara Hakushū*, 7.

30. Tonka John is a nickname Kitahara uses for his childhood self in *Memories*. Explanations of its origins differ. It is often said to be a Romanization of Kyushu dialect for the oldest son of a good family. Itō Sei, ed. *Nihon Kindai Bungaku Taikei*, vol. 59 (Kadokawa, 1969), 125.

31. Kitahara, *Omoide*, in *Hakushū Zenshū*, 2: 21.

32. Stefan Tanaka, *New Times in Modern Japan* (Princeton University Press), 2004.

33. Tanaka, *New Times in Modern Japan*, 6.

34. Tanaka, *New Times in Modern Japan*, 8.

35. Aaron Gerow, "Nation, Citizenship, and Cinema," in *A Companion to the Anthropology of Japan*, ed. Jennifer Robertson (Blackwell Publishing, 2005), 407.

36. For more on the trajectory of the Pierrot motif in Japan, including its 1960s avant-garde iterations, see Miwako Tezuka, "Experimentation and Tradition: The Avant-Garde Play *Pierrot Lunaire* by Jikken Kōbō and Takechi Tetsuji," *Art Journal* 70, no. 3 (Fall 2011): 64–86, https://www.jstor.org/stable/41430744.

37. The image is viewable at the National Gallery Prague. Shiba Kōkan, *View of the Ochanomizu Quarter in Edo*, National Gallery Prague, 1784, https://sbirky.ngprague.cz/en/dielo/CZE:NG.Vm_2596.

38. Maki Fukuoka, *The Premise of Fidelity: Science, Visuality, and Representing the Real in Nineteenth-Century Japan* (Stanford University Press, 2012), 5.

39. Fukuoka, *Premise of Fidelity*, 5.

40. Jinnai Hidenobu, *Tokyo: A Spatial Anthropology*, trans. Kimiko Nishimura (University of California Press, 1995), 107.

41. The original uses a variant character.

42. Kitahara, *Omoide*, in *Hakushū zenshū*, 2: 34.

43. Kitahara, *Omoide*, in *Hakushū Zenshū*, 2:16-17.

44. Gyewon Kim, "Registering the Real: Photography and the Emergence of New Historic Sites in Meiji Japan" (PhD diss., McGill University, 2010), https://escholarship.mcgill.ca/concern/theses/6m311p77t.

45. Kim, "Registering the Real," 5-6.
46. Kasahara Hidehiko, *"Ten'nō-sei kokka to roku-dai junkō no kinō: Meiji shoki no chihō junkō o chūshin ni:* The emperor system and the six big pilgrimages: focus on the early Meiji case," *Hōgaku kenkyū: hōritsu, seiji, shakai (Journal of law, politics, and sociology)* 93, no. 7 (2020): 1-55.
47. Kim, "Registering the Real," 26.
48. Kim, "Registering the Real," 43.
49. Kitahara, *"Jo-shi,"* in *Hakushū zenshū,* vol. 2 (Iwanami Shoten, 1984), 37-41.
50. Kitahara, "Danshō 35, 36, 37," in *Hakushū Zenshū,* vol. 2 (Iwanami Shoten, 1984), 78-80.
51. Gerow, *Visions of Japanese Modernity,* 51. Censorship and cinema will come up in the next chapter in connection with Hagiwara's poetry.
52. Gerow, *Visions of Japanese Modernity,* 51-52.
53. Gerow, *Visions of Japanese Modernity,* 45.
54. Harry Harootunian, *History's Disquiet: Modernity, Cultural Practice, and the Question Of Everyday Life* (Columbia University Press, 2000), 118.
55. Sawada Mayumi, "Kitahara Hakushū ni yoru 'Seiyō-shiki' dōyō no hihan ni tsuite," *Niijima Junior College* 27 (2007): 53-62.
56. Miki, *Kitahara Hakushū,* 378.
57. Miki, *Kitahara Hakushū,* 392.
58. Kanno Akimasa, "Mitsutsu Mizariki," in *Ishikawa Takuboku to Kitahara Hakushū,* ed. Ueda Hiroshi and Nakajima Kunihiko (Yūseidō Shuppan, 1989), 157-82.

2. Sexuality, Censorship, and State Critique in Hagiwara Sakutarō

1. See Gregory Pflugfelder, *Cartographies of Desire: Male-Male Sexuality in Japanese Discourse 1600–1950* (University of California Press, 2007); Jim Reichert, *In the Company of Men: Representations of Male-Male Sexuality in Meiji Literature* (Stanford University Press, 2006); and J. Keith Vincent, *Two-Timing Modernity: Homosocial Narrative in Modern Japanese Fiction* (Harvard University Asia Center, 2012).
2. Jonathan Abel, "Seditious Obscenity/Obscene Seditions: The Radical Eroticism of Umehara Hokumei," in *Negotiating Censorship in Modern Japan,* ed. Rachael Hutchinson (Routledge, 2013), 35-58.
3. Gregory J. Kasza, *The State and the Mass Media in Japan, 1918–1945* (University of California Press, 1993), 70.
4. For more on Kitahara's influence on *Howling at the Moon,* see Tamura Keiji, "Hagiwara Sakutarō no shi-teki shuppatsu: Hakushū taiken to sono keishō," *Taihiro Ohtani Junior College* 16 (1976): 11-22, https://doi.org/10.20682/oojc.16.0_11.
5. Harold Wright, "Poetry in Modern Japan—Some Contributions of the poet Hagiwara Sakutarō," *The Journal-Newsletter of the Association of Teachers of Japanese* 5, no. 2 (1968): 9, https://www.jstor.org/stable/488802.
6. For more on Hagiwara's post-*Howling at the Moon* career, see chapter 4 of this book.

7. Mike Sugimoto, "The Illness of Prose: Hagiwara Sakutarō and the Status of Poetry in the Modern," *Interdisciplinary Literary Studies* 4, no. 1 (Fall 2002): 22, https://www.jstor.org/stable/41208804.

8. Yasu Satoshi argues that the imagery of death and violence in Howling at the Moon situates it in its wartime context of the recent Russo-Japanese War (1904-5) and the ongoing First World War (1914-18). See Yasu Satoshi, "Hagiwara Sakutarō *Tsuki ni hoeru* to sensō," *Nihon Kindai Bungaku*, no. 98 (2018): 146-61, https://doi.org/10.19018/nihonkindaibungaku.98.0_146.

9. Hagiwara Sakutarō, "*Fūzoku kairan no shi to wa nani zo*," in *Hagiwara Sakutarō zenshū*, vol. 6, ed. Itō Shinkichi, Nakagiri Masao, Naka Tarō, Satō Fusayoshi, and Hagiwara Yōko. (Chikuma Shobō, 1975), 277.

10. Hagiwara, "*Fūzoku kairan no shi*," in *Zenshū*, vol. 6, 278-79.

11. Maki Yoshiyuki, *Fuseji no bunkashi* (Shinwasha, 2014), 108.

12. Maki, *Fuseji no bunkashi*, 110.

13. Maki, *Fuseji no bunkashi*, 107-8.

14. Maki, *Fuseji no bunkashi*, 108.

15. Tsuboi Hideto, "*Tsuki ni hoeru* wa hoe-tsuzukeru," *Saku: A Society for the Study of Hagiwara Sakutaro* 83 (May 11, 2018): 54-75.

16. Tsuboi, "Tsuki ni hoeru," 57.

17. Hagiwara Sakutarō, "Airen," in *Hagiwara Sakutarō zenshū*, vol. 1 (Chikuma Shobō, 1975), 64-65.

18. Hagiwara's use of plants to camouflage explicit sexual imagery draws on a long literary tradition. As the first poet to write a full-length book in free verse in colloquial Japanese, Hagiwara seeks fresh imagery to describe the experience of sexuality, rather than using the familiar flowers of canonical poetry. The two kinds of flowers mentioned in the poem, campanula (つりがね草, *tsurigane-sō*) and gentians (りんだう, *rindō*) are both marginal figures in the Japanese poetic canon, not literary heavyweights like chrysanthemums or morning glories. In the twentieth century, *tsurigane-sō* sometimes appeared in attempts by poets to come up with "new" autumn plants that could express the essence of fall. However, Hagiwara does not depart from the literary canon of conventional plants altogether; instead he chooses these minor plants, still connected to the Japanese literary tradition, but not freighted with as much associative weight.

19. Quoted in Umeda Jun'ichi, "*Tsuki ni hoeru* no shuppan no ikisatsu: Nihon kindai bungaku bunko kara," *Tosho no fu*, no. 3 (January 1999), http://www.lib.meiji.ac.jp/about/publication/toshonofu/tsuki3.pdf

20. Umeda, "*Tsuki ni hoeru*," n.p.

21. Janine Beichman, *Embracing the Firebird: Yosano Akiko and the Birth of the Female Voice in Modern Japanese Poetry* (University of Hawai'i Press, 2002), 190 and 202.

22. Dean A. Brink, "Situating a Badiouan Anthropocene in Hagiwara's Postnatural Poetry," *CLC Web: Comparative Literature and Culture* 16, no. 4 (December 2014): 5, https://doi.org/10.7771/1481-4374.2561.

23. Quoted in Tamura Keiji, "Hagiwara Sakutarō no shi-teki tassei: Jōsaishihen o waku to shite," *Taihiro Ōtani Tanki Daigaku Kiyō*, no. 16, (March 1979): 53-54, https://doi.org/10.20682/oojc.17.Humanities_SocialScience_43.

24. Hagiwara, "Koi o koi suru hito," in *Hagiwara Sakutarō zenshū*, vol. 1 (Chikuma Shobō, 1975), 65–66.

25. Hagiwara Sakutarō, "Hajimete Dostoevsky o yonda koro," *Hagiwara Sakutarō zenshū*, vol. 9 (Chikuma Shobō, 1976), https://www.aozora.gr.jp/cards/000067/card49852.html.

26. Kunikida Doppo, "Koi o koi suru hito," in *Nihon no tanpen shōsetsu: Meiji/Taishō* (Tokyo: Chō Shuppansha, 1973), https://www.aozora.gr.jp/cards/000038/files/327_43413.html.

27. Hagiwara's meditation on the role of nonnormative sexuality in literary production draws on his life experience of a series of passionate male friendships in the Japanese literary scene, creating a sense of autobiographical confession in these works. His letters to his mentor Kitahara often have the hopelessly one-sided passion of unrequited love, in passages like the following, from two long letters written on the same date in 1915:

"My feelings of affection toward you have now reached their peak. I have never until now felt so strange." Hagiwara Sakutarō, letter 79 to Kitahara Hakushū, in *Hagiwara Sakutarō zenshū*, vol. 13 (Chikuma Shobō, 1976), 74.

And then later that same day, in a second letter,

"Toward you, my darling, I feel a strange kind of sensation: It is like a child spoiled by his mother, like the mad pillow talk of lovers. That day at Aka-shiro Tei [a restaurant and nightlife spot in Hagiwara's hometown Maebashi, where Kitahara had visited] was when this feeling exploded. A strange and sweet, neurotic and nervous love" (76).

The preface to the collection, written by Kitahara, contains passionate language that further supports Hagiwara's attempts to unveil the repressed homoeroticism in Japanese literature. "Dear Hagiwara-kun," the epistolary preface begins, "I love you no matter what people say." Hagiwara, "*Tsuki ni hoeru,*" in *Hagiwara Sakutarō zenshū*, vol. 1 (Chikuma Shobō, 1975), 5. It is as if the preface publicly performs the love and affection Kitahara was withholding in the private letters, where he eventually attempted to parry Hagiwara's affection by setting him up in an arranged marriage.

28. Tsukimura Reiko, "Shururiarizumu no e o saki-dori shita Sakutarō no shi," *Dai 11 Kai Kokusai Nihon Bungaku Kenkyūshū-kai* 11 (November 6, 1987): 94, https://doi.org/10.24619/00002116. Also, Yasu suggests that Kawakami Tetsutarō was the first scholar to argue that this poem is actually about cinema. Yasu Satoshi, *Hagiwara Sakutarō to iu media: Hikisakareru kindai/shijin* (Mori washa, 2008), 251.

29. Aaron Gerow, *Visions of Japanese Modernity: Articulations of Cinema, Nation, and Spectatorship, 1895–1925* (University of California Press, 2010), 51.

30. Hagiwara, "Satsujin jiken," in *Hagiwara Sakutarō zenshū*, vol. 1, 33-34.

31. Shibusawa Takasuke, "Shigekiteki-na shunkan," in *Chijō Junrei Fukkokuban Bessatsu Kaisetsu* (Nihon Kindai Bungakukan, 1983), 4.

32. Quoted in Gerow, *Visions of Japanese Modernity*, 49.

33. Gerow, *Visions of Japanese Modernity*, 60.

34. Tsukimura Reiko, "Shururiarizumu," 94.

35. Cary Nelson, *Repression and Recovery: Modern American Poetry and the Politics of Cultural Memory 1910–1945* (University of Wisconsin Press, 1989), 199.

36. Suzanne W. Churchill and Adam McKible, "Little Magazines and Modernism: An Introduction," *American Periodicals* 15, no. 1 (2005): 3.

37. Hosea Hirata, *The Poetry and Poetics of Nishiwaki Junzaburō: Modernism in Translation* (Princeton University Press, 1993), 132.

38. Hirata, *Poetry and Poetics of Nishiwaki Junzaburō*, 132.

39. Itō Shinkichi, "Kanjō gurūpu ni tsuite," in *Kanjō*, ed. Itō Shinkichi (Tōji Shobō, 1961), 13.

40. Itō, "Kanjō," 13.

41. Itō, "Kanjō," 13.

42. Itō, "Kanjō," 13.

43. Itō, "Kanjō," 3.

44. Jon Holt, "In a Senchimentaru Mood: Sentimentalism in Modern Japanese Poetry and Art," *Japanese Language and Literature* 48, no. 2, (Oct. 2014): 237.

45. Hagiwara Sakutarō, "Niji o ou hito," in *Hagiwara Sakutarō zenshū*, vol. 4 (Chikuma Shobō, 1975), 454–55.

46. Toshiko Ellis, "The Topography of Dalian and the Cartography of Fantastic Asia in Anzai Fuyue's Poetry," *Comparative Literature Studies* 41, no. 4, (2004): 497, https://www.jstor.org/stable/40247445.

47. Hagiwara, "Niji o ou hito," 455.

48. Murō Saisei, *Jojōshōkyokushū*, in *Murō Saisei zenshū*, vol. 1, ed. Itō Shinkichi (Shinchōsha, 1964), 22.

49. Jeffrey Angles, *Writing the Love of Boys: Origins of Bishōnen Culture in Modernist Japanese Literature* (University of Minnesota Press, 2011), 18.

50. Murō Saisei, *Ai no shishū*, in *Murō Saisei zenshū*, vol. 2, 36.

51. Hagiwara is referring to the Asakusa Denkikan, a movie theater in the Asakusa neighborhood in Tokyo that was established in 1903. Perhaps it was this theater where he and Murō saw the crime films he was writing about.

52. Hagiwara Sakutarō, "Shokan danpen," in *Hagiwara Sakutarō zenshū*, vol. 8 (Chikuma Shobō, 1976), 165–67.

53. Edogawa Rampo, *The Edogawa Rampo Reader*, ed. and trans. Seth Jacobowitz (Kurodahan Press, 2008), 53.

54. Murō Saisei, *Jojōshōkyoushū hoi*, in *Murō Saisei zenshū*, vol. 1, 58.

3. "Fragrant Spaces Between Words": The Oblique Sexuality of Fragrance in Yonezawa Nobuko and Ōte Takuji

1. Momota Sōji, "Yonezawa Nobuko Nenpyō," in *Yonezawa Nobuko shishū*, by Yonezawa Nobuko (Dai-ichi Shobō, 1932), 382.

2. Takahashi Junko, ed., *Gendai Nihon Josei Shijin 85* (Shinshokan, 2005), 26–27.

3. Yonezawa Nobuko, "Winter House," trans. Andrew Campana, *Monkey*, accessed October 21, 13, 2021, https://monkeymagazine.org/andrew-campana.

4. Ubukata Tatsue, *Metorazaru shijin: Ōte Takuji no shōgai* (Tokyo Bijutsu, 1973), 40.

5. Yamamoto Kenkichi, *The Singing Heart: An Anthology of Japanese Poems 1900–1960*, trans. William I. Elliott and Nishihara Katsumasa (Katydid Books, 2006), 42. Original is "Soyogu gen'ei" そよぐ幻影, from *Aiiro no hiki*.

6. See Keith Vincent, *Two-Timing Modernity: Homosocial Narrative in Modern Japanese Fiction* (Harvard University Asia Center, 2012); Jim Reichert, *In the Company of Men: Representations of Male-Male Sexuality in Meiji Literature* (Stanford University Press, 2006); and Jeffrey Angles, *Writing the Love of Boys: Origins of Bishonen Culture in Modernist Japanese Literature* (University of Minnesota Press, 2011).

7. Matsuzakaya advertising circular, August 1932, quoted in "Natsuyasumi yūran nikki: Nagoyashi hakubutsukan de Yoshida Hatsusaburō-ten: 1930-Nendai Nagoya ni omoi o hasete, Matsuzakaya e," Kyū, nichiyō chō, September 4, 2014, https://foujita2003.hatenablog.com/entry/20140904/p1.

8. Shinkawa Kazue, "Watashi no naka no Ōte Takuji," in *Ōte Takuji zenshū*, vol. 4 (Haku-ou-sha, 1983), 4.

9. Ōte Takuji, "'Kōsui no hyōjō' ni tsuite: Mandanteki-na muda-banashi," in *Ōte Takuji zenshū*, vol. 5 (Haku-ou-sha, 1983), 393–403. The essay also appears in *Kaori*, ed. Tsukamoto Kunio, Nihon no meizuihitsu 48 (Sakuhinsha, 1986), https://www.aozora.gr.jp/cards/000190/card46403.html.

10. Mary Fleischer, "Incense and Decadents: Symbolist Theatre's Use of Scent," in *The Senses in Performance*, ed. Sally Banes and Andre Lepecki (Routledge, 2012), 105.

11. Walter Benjamin, "On Some Motifs in Baudelaire," in *Illuminations*, trans. Harry Zohn (New York, NY: Schocken Books: 1968), 158.

12. Julia Kristeva, *Revolution in Poetic Language*, trans. Margaret Waller (Columbia University Press, 1984), 213.

13. Brian Moeran, "Japanese Fragrance Descriptives and Gender Constructions: Preliminary Steps Towards an Anthropology of Olfaction," *Etnofoor* 18, no. 1 (2005): 97–123, https://www.jstor.org/stable/25758088.

14. Misu Yutaka, *Hana kara dōshite kōsui o tsukuru ka* (Tokuda Kōkyoku, 1912), 6–7, https://dl.ndl.go.jp/info:ndljp/pid/905476.

15. Yonezawa Nobuko, "Yoru to kunkō," in *Yonezawa Nobuko shishū* (Dai-ichi Shobō, 1937), 82–84.

16. Ōte Takuji, "Kōsui yawa," in *Ōte Takuji zenshū*, vol. 4, ed. Hara Shirō (Haku-ou-sha, 1971), 102. In manuscript form, the poem has an additional title, "Weeds to Throw at the Future: Perfume Night Story [未来へ投げる雑草：香水夜話]." The poem is included in the 1936 posthumous collection *Indigo Toad* under only its subtitle, "Perfume Night Story," and it is more commonly anthologized this way (4: 762n33).

17. Rachel Blau de Plessis, *Blue Studios* (University of Alabama Press, 2006), 81–82.

18. Blau de Plessis, *Blue Studios,* 106.

19. Yonezawa Nobuko, "Hisomeru yume," in *Yonezawa Nobuko shishū* (Dai-ichi Shobō, 1937), 25.

20. Yonezawa Nobuko, "Sōzō," in *Yonezawa Nobuko shishū* (Dai-ichi Shobō, 1937),132–33.

21. Yonezawa Nobuko, "Jūgatsu no veranda," in *Yonezawa Nobuko shishū* (Dai-ichi Shobō, 1937), 72–74.

22. Deborah Shamoon, *Passionate Friendship: The Aesthetics of Girls' Culture in Japan* (University of Hawai'i Press, 2011), 33.

23. Shamoon, *Passionate Friendship*, 33.
24. Ōte Takuji, *Ōte Takuji zenshū*, 1:309.

4. *Ice Land* and *Black Cypress*: Lyric Poetry and Photography in a Time of Total War

1. André Lefevre, "Slauerhoff and 'Po Tsju I': Three Paradigms for the Study of Influence," *Tamkang Review* 10 no. 1 (1979): 75.
2. Theodor Adorno, "On Lyric Poetry and Society," in *Notes to Literature Vol. 1*, trans. Shierry Weber Nicholsen (Columbia University Press, 1991), 45.
3. Anne-Lise François, *Open Secrets: The Literature of Uncounted Experience* (Stanford University Press, 2008), 135–36.
4. Charles Fox, "Free Verse in the Taishō Era," in *The Columbia Companion to Modern East Asian Literature*, ed. Joshua S. Mostow, Kirk A. Denton, Bruce Fulton, and Sharalyn Orbaugh (Columbia University Press, 2003), 148.
5. Nakano Toshio, *Nihon no shiika to sensō: Hakushū to minshū, sōryoku-sen e no michi* (NHK Books, 2012).
6. Tsuboi Hideto, "Modern Poetry, Popular Song, and Their Dangerous Liaisons," trans. Alexander Murphy, *Japan Forum* 30, no. 3 (2018): 323, https://doi.org/10.1080/09555803.2018.1427775.
7. Tsuboi Hideto, "Kokugo, kokushi, kokumin shijin: Kitahara Hakushū to Hagiwara Sakutarō," *Bungaku* 9, no. 4 (1998): 65.
8. Tsuboi, "Kokugo, kokushi, kokumin shijin," 65.
9. Masako Hashimoto, "Beyond Character Consumerism. A Manga Adaptation of Can't be Howlin' at the Moon and the Problem of War Poetry," in *Japan's Contemporary Media Culture: Between Local and Global*, ed. Martin Roth, Hiroshi Yoshida, and Martin Picard (Cross-Asia E-Books, 2021), 75, https://doi.org/10.11588/crossasia.971.
10. A more literal English translation of the title *Kurohi* is "Thuja Sandishii" or "Japanese Arborvitae," but I have followed Fukasawa in translating it as *Black Cypress*.
11. Theodor Adorno, "Late Style in Beethoven," trans. Susan H. Gillespie, in *Essays on Music*, ed. Richard D. Leppert and Susan H. Gillespie (University of California Press, 2002), 566.
12. Edward W. Said, *On Late Style: Music and Literature Against the Grain* (Pantheon Books, 2006).
13. This retreat overlaps with the phenomenon of apostasy found in *tenkō* (転向) literature, wherein formerly committed leftist writers produced nationalistic literature during the 1930s. Unlike the *tenkō* writers, who were originally Marxists, anarchists, and other leftists, Hagiwara was not ideologically affiliated prior to their 1930s. For more on the *tenkō* phenomenon among leftist Japanese poets, see Miriam Silverberg, *Changing Song: The Marxist Manifestos of Nakano Shigeharu* (Princeton University Press, 1990).
14. Margaret Benton Fukasawa, *Kitahara Hakushū: His Life and Poetry* (Cornell University Press, 1993), 162.
15. Makoto Ueda, *Modern Japanese Poets and the Nature of Literature* (Stanford University Press, 1983), 148–49.

16. Fukasawa, *Kitahara Hakushū*, 159.
17. Kitahara Hakushū, *Kurohi*, in *Hakushū zenshū*, vol. 12, ed. Kimata Osamu (Iwanami Shoten, 1985), 142.
18. Hagiwara Sakutarō, *Hyōtō*, in *Hagiwara Sakutarō zenshū*, vol. 2 (Chikuma Shobō, 1976), 103–104.
19. Kitahara Hakushū, *Kurohi*, in *Hakushū zenshū*, vol. 12, ed. Kimata Osamu (Iwanami Shoten, 1985), 5.
20. Hakushū, *Kurohi*, in *Hakushū zenshū*, 12: 130.
21. Donald Keene, *World Within Walls: A History of Japanese Literature*, vol. 1 (Columbia University Press, 1999), 507.
22. Hagiwara Sakutarō, *Hagiwara Sakutarō shashin sakuhin: Nosutarujia shijin ga totta mō hitotsu no fūkei* (Shinchōsha, 1999), 85.
23. Hagiwara, *Hagiwara Sakutarō shashin sakuhin*, 68–69.
24. Although Hagiwara's pairs of photographs are usually identical, it is interesting to note that this pair contains small differences, so that the right-hand edge of each image is cropped a little differently. This creates a sense of rupture or disjunction—indeed it's possible that this piece might not show up correctly when viewed in the stereoscope.
25. Hagiwara Sakutarō, *Hyōtō*, in *Hagiwara Sakutarō zenshū*, 2:120–121.
26. Kitahara, *Kurohi*, in *Hakushū zenshū*, 12: 14.

5. Oral Culture and the Poetry of Officially Licensed State Critique

1. Margaret Helen Persin, *Getting the Picture: The Ekphrastic Principle in Twentieth-Century Spanish Poetry* (Associated University Presses, 1997), 187.
2. Gregory J. Kasza, *The State and the Mass Media in Japan 1918–1945* (University of California Press, 1988), 76.
3. Kasza, *State and the Mass Media in Japan*, 92.
4. Tsuboi Hideto, *Koe no shukusai: Nihon kindaishi to sensō* (Nagoya University Press, 1997), 35.
5. Tsuboi, *Koe no shukusai*, 162.
6. Jonathan Culler, *Theory of the Lyric* (Harvard University Press, 2015), 336–37.
7. Tsuboi, *Koe no shukusai*, 238.
8. Mike Sugimoto, "Nation as Artwork: The Modernist Aesthetics and Poetics of Hagiwara Sakutarō," *National Identities* 5, vol. 2 (July 2003): 182, https://doi.org/10.1080/1460894032000124411
9. National Diet Library, "Kitahara Hakushū jisaku rōdoku," performed by Kitahara Hakushū Columbia Records, Rekishiteki Ongen Sound Archive, 1939, streaming sound file, http://rekion.dl.ndl.go.jp/info:ndljp/pid/3571476?itemId=info%3Andljp%2Fpid%2F3571476&__lang=en.
10. Kitahara Hakushū, "*Danshō* 22," in *Hakushū zenshū*, vol. 2, ed. Nakajima Kunihiko (Iwanami Shoten, 1985), 73–74.
11. Kitahara, "*Danshō* 22," 73–74.
12. Kitahara Hakushū, "*In'ei*," in *Hakushū zenshū*, vol. 2, ed. Nakajima Kunihiko (Iwanami Shoten, 1985), 99.

13. National Diet Library, "Shi rōdoku: Nogizaka kurabu, Hi, Numazu Chihō," performed by Hagiwara Sakutarō, Columbia Records, Rekishiteki Ongen Sound Archive, 1940, streaming sound file, http://rekion.dl.ndl.go.jp/info:ndljp/pid/3571577.

14. Hagiwara Sakutarō, *Hyōtō*, in *Hagiwara Sakutarō zenshū*, vol. 2 (Chikuma Shobō, 1975), 110-11.

15. Hagiwara, *Hyōtō*, 104.

16. Isoda Kōichi, "*Hyōtō* no shūhen: Hagiwara Sakutarō (11)," *Gunzō* 41, No. 12 (1986): 220.

17. Isoda, "*Hyōtō* no shūhen," 222.

18. Yasu Satoshi, *Hagiwara Sakutarō to iu media: hiki-sakareru kindai/shijin* (Mori wa sha, 2008).

19. For example, in 1908, when the Yokota Film Studio was forbidden to screen a French film about the trial and execution of Louis XVI during the French Revolution, the *benshi* at a theater in the Kanda area of Tokyo adjusted their scripts so that King Louis XVI was now an American bandit king, and the populist mob calling for his death were enthusiastic citizens helping the state to capture him. Of course, while many audience members were probably happy to go along with the edited story line, it is highly likely that at least a few were in on the joke, and that audiences managed to catch the revolutionary thrust of the film's scenes of populist mobilization. Satō Tadao, *Nihon eiga shi*, vol. 1 (Iwanami Shoten, 1995), 101.

20. Aaron Gerow, *Visions of Japanese Modernity: Cinema, Nation, and Spectatorship 1995–1925* (University of California Press, 2010), 152.

21. For example, the popular late-1920s Tokyo *benshi* Ōkura Mitsugu (1899-1978) was famed for his ability to bring eroticism and sexuality to his narration of even the most innocuous films approved by the censors, so that, in the words of one disapproving letter to the editor in 1928, "Any film, no matter the film, whether a tale of patriotism and loyalty, or a tale of maternal love, becomes a work of obscenity." Satō, *Nihon eiga shi*, 1: 316-17.

22. Hagiwara Sakutarō, "Kokumin shi ni tsuite," in *Hagiwara Sakutarō zenshū*, vol. 6 (Chikuma Shobō, 1975), 509-10. Original appeared in *Miyako shinbun*, February 2, 3, and 4, 1942. Then it was reprinted in Kawaji Ryūkō, ed., *Dai Nippon Shishū: Sei Sen ni Utau* (Ōbunsha, 1942), 226-27.

23. Tsuboi Hideto makes the point that Hagiwara was the most famous poet to appear in this particular collection, making his essay a point of prestige, a way to make the propagandistic book look more like serious literature (Tsuboi, *Koe no shukusai*, 177).

24. An analysis of the language used by *benshi* appears in Satō, *Nihon eiga shi*, 1: 103-104.

25. See Masako Hashimoto, "Beyond Character Consumerism: A Manga Adaptation of Can't be Howlin' at the Moon and the Problem of War Poetry," in *Japan's Contemporary Media Culture Between Local and Global: Content, Practice, and Theory*, ed. Martin Roth, Hiroshi Yoshida, and Martin Picard (Cross Asia E-Books, 2021), 75.

26. Hagiwara, *"Kokumin shi ni tsuite,"* in *Hagiwara Sakutarō Zenshū*, vol. 6, ed. Itō Shinkichi, Nakagiri Masao, Naka Tarō, Satō Fusayoshi, and Hagiwara Yōko, (Chikuma Shobō, 1975), 509.
27. Quoted in Satō, *Nihon eiga shi*, 1: 315.
28. Hagiwara Sakutarō, "Buster Keaton," in *Hagiwara Sakutarō zenshū*, vol. 5 (Chikuma Shobō, 1977), 276–77.
29. Hagiwara, "Buster Keaton," 276.
30. Hagiwara, "Buster Keaton," 276.
31. Iijima Kōichi, *Hagiwara Sakutarō* (Kadokawa Shoten, 1975), 39.
32. Iijima, *Hagiwara Sakutarō*, 39.
33. Hagiwara, "Buster Keaton," 278.
34. Hagiwara, *Hyōtō*, 108.

Conclusion: "Poetry Gods" and the Legacy of Officially Licensed Poetry

1. Yonezawa Nobuko, "Sōzō," in *Yonezawa Nobuko shishū* (Dai-ichi Shobō, 1937), 132–33.
2. Tamura Ryūichi, "Shishin," in *Tamura Ryūichi zenshū*, vol 1., ed. Hasegawa Ikuo, (Kawade Shobō Shinsha, 2010), 149.
3. More about Arechi appears in Kitagawa Tōru's *Arechi ron* (Shichōsha, 1983); Kuroda Saburō's "'Arechi' ron" in *Gendaishinyūmon*, ed. Kuroda Saburō, Shichōsha, 1969), 233–69; and Tamura Ryūichi's *Wakai Arechi* (Kodansha, 2007).
4. Tamura Ryūichi, "Shishin," in *Tamura Ryūichi Zenshū*, vol. 1, ed. Hasegawa Ikuo, (Kawade Shobō Shinsha, 2010),149.
5. Christopher Drake, "Introduction to *Dead Languages*," in *Tamura Ryuichi: On the Life and Work of a 20th Century Master*, ed. Takako Lento and Wayne Miller (Pleiades Press, 2011), 74.

Bibliography

Abel, Jonathan. "Seditious Obscenity/Obscene Seditions: The Radical Eroticism of Umehara Hokumei." In *Negotiating Censorship in Modern Japan*, edited by Rachael Hutchinson. Routledge, 2013.

Adorno, Theodor. "Late Style in Beethoven," translated by Susan H. Gillespie. In *Essays on Music*, edited by Richard D. Leppert and Susan H. Gillespie. University of California Press, 2002.

Adorno, Theodor. *Notes to Literature Vol. 1*, translated by Shierry Weber Nicholsen. Columbia University Press, 1991.

Angles, Jeffrey. *Writing the Love of Boys: Origins of Bishonen Culture in Modernist Japanese Literature*. University of Minnesota Press, 2011.

Atkins, Paul S. *Teika: The Life and Works of a Medieval Japanese Poet*. University of Hawai'i Press, 2017.

Beichman, Janine. *Embracing the Firebird: Yosano Akiko and the Birth of the Female Voice in Modern Japanese Poetry*. University of Hawai'i Press, 2002.

Benjamin, Walter. *Illuminations*, translated by Harry Zohn. Schocken Books, 1969.

Blau de Plessis, Rachel. *Blue Studios*. University of Alabama Press, 2006.

Bourdaghs, Michael. *The Dawn That Never Comes: Shimazaki Tōson and Japanese Nationalism*. Columbia University Press, 2003.

Brink, Dean A. "Situating a Badiouan Anthropocene in Hagiwara's Postnatural Poetry." *CLC Web: Comparative Literature and Culture* 16, no. 4 (December 2014): article 5.

Bush, Christopher. *Ideographic Modernism: China, Writing, Media*. Oxford University Press, 2010.

Burns, Susan L. "Constructing the Body: Health and the Nation in Nineteenth-Century Japan." In *Nation Work: Asian Elites and National Identities*, edited by Timothy Brook and André Schmid, University of Michigan Press, 2000.

Churchill, Suzanne W. and Adam McKible. "Little Magazines and Modernism: An Introduction." *American Periodicals* 15, no. 1, (2005): 1–5.

Culler, Jonathan. *Theory of the Lyric*. Harvard University Press, 2015.

Doak, Kevin. *Dreams of Difference: The Japan Romantic School and the Crisis of Modernity*. University of California Press, 1994.

Drake, Christopher. "Introduction to *Dead Languages*." In *Tamura Ryuichi: On the Life and Work of a 20th Century Master*, edited by Takako Lento and Wayne Miller. Pleiades Press, 2011.

Edogawa, Rampo. *The Edogawa Rampo Reader*, edited and translated by Seth Jacobowitz. Kurodahan Press, 2008.

Ellis, Toshiko. "The Topography of Dalian and the Cartography of Fantastic Asia in Anzai Fuyue's Poetry." *Comparative Literature Studies* 41, no. 4 (2004): 482–500.
Fenves, Peter. "Benjamin, Studying, China: Toward a Universal 'Universism.'" *positions: asia critique* 26, no. 1 (February 2018): 35–57.
Fleischer, Mary. "Incense and Decadents: Symbolist Theatre's Use of Scent." In *The Senses in Performance*, edited by Sally Barnes and Andre Lepecki. Routledge, 2012.
Fox, Charles. "Free Verse in the Taishō Era." In *The Columbia Companion to Modern East Asian Literature*, edited by Joshua S. Mostow, Kirk A. Denton, Bruce Fulton, and Sharalyn Orbaugh. Columbia University Press, 2003.
François, Anne-Lise. *Open Secrets: The Literature of Uncounted Experience*. Stanford University Press, 2008.
Fukasawa, Margaret Benton. *Kitahara Hakushū: His Life and Poetry*. Cornell University Press, 1993.
Fukunaga Takehiko. *Haishi*. In *Fukunaga Takehiko Denshi zenshū*. Vol. 5. Shōgakukan eBooks, 2019.
Fukuoka, Maki. *The Premise of Fidelity: Science, Visuality, and Representing the Real in Nineteenth-Century Japan*. Stanford University Press, 2012.
Gardner, William. *Advertising Tower: Japanese Modernism and Modernity in the 1920s*. Harvard University Asia Center, 2006.
Gerow, Aaron. "Nation, Citizenship, and Cinema." In *A Companion to the Anthropology of Japan*, edited by Jennifer Robertson. Blackwell Publishing, 2005.
Gerow, Aaron. *Visions of Japanese Modernity: Articulations of Cinema, Nation, and Spectatorship, 1895–1925*. University of California Press, 2010.
Hagiwara Sakutarō. *Hagiwara Sakutarō shashin sakuhin: Nosutarujia Shijin ga Totta Mō Hitotsu no Fūkei*. Tokyo: Shinchōsha, 1999.
Hagiwara Sakutarō. *Hagiwara Sakutarō zenshū*. Volumes 1–6, 8, 9, 13. Chikuma Shobō, 1977.
Hagiwara Sakutarō. "Nankin kanraku no hi ni." *Asahi Shimbun*. December 13, 1937.
Hagiwara Sakutarō. *Tsuki ni hoeru*. In *Gendaishi Bunko 1009: Hagiwara Sakutarō*. Shichōsha, 1975. https://www.aozora.gr.jp/cards/000067/files/859_21656.html.
Harootunian, H. D. "Between Politics and Culture: Authority and the Ambiguities of Intellectual Choice in Imperial Japan." In *Japan in Crisis: Essays on Taishō Democracy*, edited by H. D. Harootunian and Bernard Silverman. Princeton University Press, 1974.
Harootunian, H. D. *History's Disquiet: Modernity, Cultural Practice, and the Question of Everyday Life*. Columbia University Press, 2000.
Hashimoto, Masako. "Beyond Character Consumerism: A Manga Adaptation of *Can't be Howlin' at the Moon* and the Problem of War Poetry." In *Japan's Contemporary Media Culture Between Local and Global: Content, Practice, and Theory*, edited by Martin Roth, Hiroshi Yoshida, and Martin Picard. Cross Asia E-Books, 2021.
Hirata, Hosea. *The Poetry and Poetics of Nishiwaki Junzaburō: Modernism in Translation*. Princeton University Press, 2016.

Holt, Jon. "In a Senchimentaru Mood: Sentimentalism in Modern Japanese Poetry and Art." *Japanese Language and Literature* 48 no. 2 (October 2014): 237–78.
Hozumi Akiyuki. "Tozasareta mura de 5 nin no josei o satsugai … naizō o eguri totta otoko no 'hontō no nerai.'" *Gendai Bijinesu*. September 26, 2020. https://gendai.ismedia.jp/articles/-/75896.
Iijima Kōichi, *Hagiwara Sakutarō*. Kadokawa Shoten, 1975.
Inoue Testusjirō, Toyama Masakazu, and Yatabe Ryōkichi. *Shintaishishō*. 1st ed. Maruyazen, 1882. https://dl.ndl.go.jp/info:ndljp/pid/876377.
Isoda Kōichi, "*Hyōtō* no shūhen: Hagiwara Sakutarō (11)." *Gunzō* 41, no. 12 (1986): 216–31.
Itō Sei, ed. *Nihon Kindai Bungaku Taikei*. Vol. 59. Kadokawa, 1969.
Itō Shinkichi, ed. *Kanjō*. Tōji Shobō, 1961.
Itō Shinkichi. *Itō Shinkichi chosakushū*. Vol. 6. Chūsekisha, 2001.
Ivy, Marilyn. *Discourses of the Vanishing*. University of Chicago Press, 1995.
Jackson, Earl. "The Heresy of Meaning: Japanese Symbolist Poetry." *Harvard Journal of Asiatic Studies* 51, no. 2 (Dec. 1991): 561–98.
Jinnai Hidenobu. *Tokyo: A Spatial Anthropology*, translated by Kimiko Nishimura. University of California Press, 1995.
Johnson, Barbara, "Teaching Deconstructively." In *The Barbara Johnson Reader: The Surprise of Otherness*, edited by Melissa Feuerstein, Bill Johnson González, Lili Porten, and Keja L. Valens. Duke University Press, 2014.
Kanno Akimasa, "Mitsutsu Mizariki." In *Ishikawa Takuboku to Kitahara Hakushū*, edited by Ueda Hiroshi and Nakajima Kunihiko. Yūseidō Shuppan, 1989.
Kasahara Hidehiko, "Ten'nō-sei kokka to roku-dai junkō no kinō: Meiji shoki no chihō junkō o chūshin ni." *Hōgaku kenkyū: hōritsu, seiji, shakai* 93, no. 7 (2020): 1-55.
Kasza, Gregory J. *The State and the Mass Media in Japan 1918–1945*. University of California Press, 1988.
Kaufman, Robert. "Aura, Still." *October* 99 (Winter 2002): 45–80.
Kawaji Ryūkō, ed. *Dai Nippon shishū: Sei sen ni utau*. Ōbunsha, 1942.
Kawamoto Saburō. *Hakushū bōkei*. Shinshokan, 2012.
Keene, Donald. *World Within Walls: A History of Japanese Literature*. Vol. 1. Columbia University Press, 1999.
Kim, Gyewon. "Registering the Real: Photography and the Emergence of New Historic Sites in Meiji Japan." PhD diss., McGill University, 2010. https://escholarship.mcgill.ca/concern/theses/6m311p77t.
Kinoshita Mokutarō. *Kinoshita Mokutarō zenshū*. Volume 13. Iwanami Shoten, 1982.
Kitagawa Tōru. *Arechi ron*. Shichōsha, 1983.
Kitahara Hakushū, *Chijō Junrei Fukkokuban*. Nihon Kindai Bungakukan, 1983.
Kitahara Hakushū. *Kashū Kurohi*. Tanka Shimbunsha Bunko, 1994. https://www.aozora.gr.jp/cards/000106/files/52301_54415.html.
Kitahara Hakushū. *Kitahara Hakushū zenkashū*. Vol. 1. Iwanami Shoten, 1990.
Kitahara Hakushū. *Kitahara Hakushū zenkashū*. Vol. 3. Iwanami Shoten, 1990.
Kitahara Hakushū. *Kitahara Hakushū zenshū*. Iwanami Shoten, Volumes 1, 2, and 12. 1985.

Kitahara Hakushū. "Ōkawa Fūkei." In *Dai Tōkyō Hanjōki*. Vol. 1. *Shitamachi-hen*, Akutagawa Ryūnosuke, Izumi Kyōka, Kitahara Hakushū, Yoshii Isamu, Kubota Mantarō, Tayama Katai, and Kishida Ryūsei. Kodansha, 2013.

Kitahara Hakushū. *Omoide: Jojōshōkyoku-shū*. Nihon Tosho Sentā, 1999.

Kondō Yōta. "Sensō-shi no jōken." *Gendai Shi Techō* 5 (2001): 40–47.

Kunikida Doppō. "Koi o koi suru hito." In *Nihon no tanpen shōsetsu: Meiji/Taishō*. Chō Shuppansha, 1973. https://www.aozora.gr.jp/cards/000038/files/327_43413.html.

Kim, Gyewon. "Registering the Real: Photography and the Emergence of New Historic Sites in Meiji Japan." PhD diss., McGill University, 2010. https://escholarship.mcgill.ca/concern/theses/6m311p77t.

Kristeva, Julia. *Revolution in Poetic Language*, translated by Margaret Waller. Columbia University Press, 1984.

Kuroda Saburō, ed. *Gendaishinyūmon*. Shichōsha, 1969.

Kyusojin Hitaku, ed. *Kokinshū*. Kyuko Shoin, 1991. http://jti.lib.virginia.edu/japanese/kokinshu/kikokin.html.

Lefevre, André. "Slauerhoff and 'Po Tsju I': Three Paradigms for the Study of Influence." *Tamkang Review* 10, no. 1 (1979): 72–80.

Lento, Takako, and Wayne Miller, eds. *Tamura Ryuichi: On the Life and Work of a Twentieth-Century Master*. Pleiades Press, 2011.

Mackie, Vera, and Susumu Yamaizumi. "Introduction." In *Japan and the High Treason Incident*, edited by Masako Gavin and Ben Middleton. Routledge, 2013.

Maeda Ai. *Text and The City: Essays on Japanese Modernity*, edited by James A. Fujii. Duke University Press, 2004.

Maki Yoshiyuki. *Fuseji no bunkashi*. Shinwasha, 2014.

Mehl, Scott. *The Ends of Meter in Modern Japanese Poetry: Translation and Form*. Cornell University Press, 2022.

Miki Taku. *Kitahara Hakushū*. Chikuma Shobo, 2005.

Misu Yutaka. *Hana kara dōshite kōsui o tsukuru ka*. Tokuda Kōkyoku, 1912. https://dl.ndl.go.jp/info:ndljp/pid/905476.

Miyazaki Koshoshi, Tayama Katai, Matsuoka Kunio, Saganoya Omuro, and Kunikida Doppo, *Jojōshi*. Edited by Miyazaki Kokoshi. Tōji Shobō, 1964.

Miyoshi Yukio. *Kindai no jojō*. Hanawa Shobo, 1990.

Moeran, Brian. "Japanese Fragrance Descriptives and Gender Constructions: Preliminary Steps Towards an Anthropology of Olfaction." *Etnofoor* 18, no. 1 (2005): 97–123.

Morita, James R. "The *Jojōshi*." *Journal of the Association of Teachers of Japanese* 10, no. 2/3 (September 1975): 179–200.

Murō Saisei. *Jojōshōkyokushū*. In *Murō Saisei zenshū*, vol. 1. Edited by Itō Shinkichi. Shinchōsha, 1964.

Murō Saisei and Hagiwara Sakutarō. *Ni kon ittai no tomo*. Chūokoran shinsha, 2021.

Nakano Toshio. *Nihon no shiika to sensō: Hakushū to minshū, sōryoku-sen e no michi*. NHK Books, 2012.

Nakamura Shin'ichirō. *Waga kokoro no shijin-tachi: Tōson, Hakushū, Sakutarō, Tatsuji*. Ushio, 1998.

National Diet Library. "Kitahara Hakushū jisaku rōdoku." Performed by Kitahara Hakushū. 1939. Rekishiteki Ongen Sound Archive. Streaming sound file. http://rekion.dl.ndl.go.jp/info:ndljp/pid/3571476?itemId=info%3Andljp%2Fpid%2F3571476&__lang=en.

National Diet Library. "Shi Rōdoku: Nogizaka Kurabu, Hi, Numazu Chihō." Performed by Hagiwara Sakutarō. 1940. Rekishiteki Ongen Sound Archive. Streaming sound file. http://rekion.dl.ndl.go.jp/info:ndljp/pid/3571577.

"Natsuyasumi yūran nikki: Nagoyashi hakubutsukan de Yoshida Hatsusaburō-ten: 1930-Nendai Nagoya ni omoi o hasete, Matsuzakaya e." Kyū, nichiyō chō. September 4, 2014. https://foujita2003.hatenablog.com/entry/20140904/p1.

Nealon, Christopher. "The Poetic Case." *Critical Inquiry* 33, no. 4 (Summer 2007): 865–86.

Nelson, Cary. *Repression and Recovery: Modern American Poetry and the Politics of Cultural Memory 1910–1945*. University of Wisconsin Press, 1989.

Ōte Takuji. "'Kōsui no hyōjō' ni tsuite: Mandanteki-na muda-banashi." In *Kaori*, edited by Tsukamoto Kunio. Nihon no meizuihitsu 48. Sakuhin-sha, 1986. https://www.aozora.gr.jp/cards/000190/card46403.html.

Ōte Takuji. *Ōte Takuji shishū*. Sōgensha, 1948.

Ōte Takuji. *Ōte Takuhji zenshū*. 6 vols. Edited by Hara Shirō. Tokyo: Haku-ou-sha, 1970–71.

Ōte Takuji. *Sekai no shi 28: Ōte Takuji shishū*. Yayoi Shobo. 1965, https://www.aozora.gr.jp/cards/000190/files/1029_20618.html.

Persin, Margaret Helen. *Getting the Picture: The Ekphrastic Principle in Twentieth-Century Spanish Poetry*. Associated University Presses, 1997.

Pflugfelder, Gregory. *Cartographies of Desire: Male-Male Sexuality in Japanese Discourse 1600–1950*. University of California Press, 2007.

Rabson, Steve. *Righteous Cause or Tragic Folly: Changing Views of War in Modern Japanese Poetry*. University of Michigan Center for Japanese Studies, 1998.

Reichert, Jim. *In the Company of Men: Representations of Male-Male Sexuality in Meiji Literature*. Stanford University, 2006.

Rodd, Laurel C., and Mary Henkenius, trans. and eds. *Kokinshū: A Collection of Poems Ancient and Modern*. Cheng And Tsui, 1996.

Said, Edward W. *On Late Style: Music and Literature Against the Grain*. Pantheon Books, 2006.

Sand, Jordan. *House and Home in Modern Japan: Architecture, Domestic Space, and Bourgeois Culture*. Harvard University Asia Center, 2003.

Sas, Miryam. *Fault Lines: Cultural Memory and Japanese Surrealism*. Stanford University Press, 1999.

Satō Isao. *Eishi to Nihon shijin*. Hokuseido Press, 1982.

Satō Tadao. *Nihon eiga shi*. Vol. 1. Iwanami Shoten, 1995.

Sawada Mayumi. "Kitahara Hakushū ni yoru 'Seiyō-shiki' dōyō no hihan ni tsuite." *Niijima Junior College* 27 (2007): 53–62.

Schulz, Evelyn. "Narratives of Counter-Modernity: Urban Spaces and Mnemonic Sites in the "Tōkyō Hanjōki." *European Journal of East Asian Studies* 2, no. 1 (2003) 117–51.

Sedgwick, Eve Kosofsky. *Epistemology of the Closet*. University of California, 1990.
Sedgwick, Eve Kosofsky. *Tendencies*. Duke University Press, 1993.
Senuma Shigeki, ed. *Chijō junrei fukkoku ban*. Nihon Kindai Bungakukan, 1983.
Shamoon, Deborah. *Passionate Friendship: The Aesthetics of Girl's Culture in Japan*. University of Hawai'i Press, 2012.
Shiba Kōkan. *View of the Ochanomizu Quarter in Edo*. National Gallery Prague. 1784. https://sbirky.ngprague.cz/en/dielo/CZE:NG.Vm_2596.
Shibusawa Takasuke. "Shigekiteki-na shunkan." In *Chijō Junrei Fukkokuban Bessatsu Kaisetsu*. Nihon Kindai Bungakukan, 1983.
Silverberg, Miriam. *Changing Song: The Marxist Manifestos of Nakano Shigeharu*. Princeton University Press, 1990.
Smits, Ivo. "The Poet and the Politician: Teika and the Compilation of the Shinchokusenshū." *Monumenta Nipponica* 53, no. 4 (Winter 1998): 427–72.
Stalling, Jonathan. *The Poetics of Emptiness: Transformations of Asian Thought in American Poetry*. Fordham University Press, 2011.
Sugimoto, Mike. "The Illness of Prose: Hagiwara Sakutarō and the Status of Poetry in the Modern." *Interdisciplinary Literary Studies* 4, no. 1 (Fall 2002): 20–37.
Sugimoto, Mike. "Nation as Artwork: The Modernist Aesthetics and Poetics of Hagiwara Sakutarō." *National Identities* 5, no. 2 (July 2003): 179–92.
Takagai Hiroya. *Hakushū*. Shoshi Yamada, 2008.
Takahata Isao, dir. *Yanagawa Horiwari monogatari*. 1987. Nibariki/Studio Ghibli. https://archive.org/details/Yanagawa-Horiwari-Monogatari.
Takahashi Junko, ed. *Gendai Nihon josei shijin 85*. Shinshokan, 2005.
Tamura Keiji, "Hagiwara Sakutarō no shi-teki shuppatsu: Hakushū taiken to sono keishō," *Taihiro Ohtani Junior College* 16 (1976): 11–22, https://doi.org/10.20682/oojc.16.0_11.
Tamura Keiji, "Hagiwara Sakutarō no shi-teki tassei: Jōsai-shihen o waku to shite." *Taihiro Ōtani Tanki Daigaku Kiyō*, no. 16 (March 1979): 43–57.
Tamura Ryūichi. *Shijin no nōto*. Kodansha, 2004.
Tamura Ryūichi. *Tamura Ryūichi Zenshū*, vol. 1. Edited by Hasegawa Ikuo. Kawade Shobō Shinsha, 2010.
Tamura Ryūichi. *Wakai arechi*. Kodansha, 2007.
Tanaka, Stefan. *New Times in Modern Japan*. Princeton University Press, 2006.
Tatsumi, Takayuki. *Full Metal Apache: Transactions Between Cyberpunk Japan and Avant-Pop America*. Duke University Press, 2006.
Tezuka, Miwako. "Experimentation and Tradition: The Avant-Garde Play *Pierrot Lunaire* by Jikken Kōbō and Takechi Tetsuji." *Art Journal* 70, no. 3 (Fall 2011): 64–86.
Tipton, Elise K. *Modern Japan: A Social and Political History*. Routledge, 2008.
Torii Kazu, ed. *Matsuzakaya hyakunen shi*. Matsuzakaya, 2010.
Tsuboi Hideto. *Koe no shukusai: Nihon kindaishi to sensō*. Nagoya University Press, 1997.
Tsuboi Hideto. "Kokugo, kokushi, kokumin shijin: Kitahara Hakushū to Hagiwara Sakutarō." *Bungaku* 9, no. 4 (1998): 56–68.

Tsuboi Hideto. "Modern Poetry, Popular Song, and Their Dangerous Liaisons," translated by Alexander Murphy. *Japan Forum* 30, no. 3 (2018): 313-36.

Tsuboi Hideto. "*Tsuki ni hoeru* wa hoe-tsuzukeru." *Saku: A Society for the Study of Hagiwara Sakutaro* 83, May 11, 2018: 54-75.

Tsukimura Reiko. "Shurearizumu no e o saki Torishita Sakutarō no shi." *Dai 11 Kai Kokusai Nihon Bungaku Kenkyūshū-kai* (November 6, 1987): 87-102.

Tsvetaeva, Marina. *Art in the Light of Conscience: Eight Essays on Poetry*, translated by Angela Livingstone. Bloodaxe Books, 2010.

Tuck, Robert. *Idly Scribbling Rhymers: Poetry, Print and Community in Nineteenth-Century Japan*. Columbia University Press, 2018.

Ubukata Tatsue. *Metorazaru shijin: Ōte Takuji no shōgai*. Tokyo Bijutsu, 1973.

Ueda Hiroshi and Nakajima Kunihiko. *Ishikawa Takuboku to Kitahara Hakushū*. Yūseidō Shuppan, 1989.

Ueda Makoto. *Modern Japanese Poets and the Nature of Literature*. Stanford University Press, 1983.

Umeda Jun'ichi. "*Tsuki ni hoeru* no shuppan no ikisatsu: Nihon kindai bungaku bunko kara," *Tosho no fu*, no. 3 (January 1999). http://www.lib.meiji.ac.jp/about/publication/toshonofu/tsuki3.pdf.

Vincent, Keith. *Two-Timing Modernity: Homosocial Narrative in Modern Japanese Fiction*. Harvard University Asia Center, 2012.

Wang, David Der-Wei. *The Lyrical in Epic Time: Modern Chinese Intellectuals and Artists Through the 1949 Crisis*. Columbia University Press, 2015.

White, Merry. *Coffee Life in Japan*. University of California Press, 2012.

Wright, Harold. "Poetry in Modern Japan—Some Contributions of the Poet Hagiwara Sakutarō." *The Journal-Newsletter of the Association of Teachers of Japanese* 5, no. 2 (1968): 9-16.

Yamamoto Kenkichi. *The Singing Heart: An Anthology of Japanese Poems 1900-1960*, translated by William I. Elliott and Nishihara Katsumasa. Katydid Books, 2006.

Yasu Satoshi. "Hagiwara Sakutarō *Tsuki ni hoeru* to sensō." *Nihon Kindai Bungaku*, no. 98 (2018): 146-61.

Yasu Satoshi. *Hagiwara Sakutarō to iu media: Hikisakareru kindai/shijin*. Mori Washa, 2008.

Yonezawa Nobuko. "Winter House," translated by Andrew Campana. *Monkey*. Accessed October 13, 2021. https://monkeymagazine.org/andrew-campana.

Yonezawa Nobuko. *Yonezawa Nobuko shishū*. Dai-ichi Shobō, 1932.

Yoshii Isamu, Akutagawa Ryūnosuke, Izumi Kyōka, Kitahara Hakushū, Kubota Mantarō, Tayama Katai, and Kishida Ryūsei. *Dai Tōkyō hanjōki*. Kodansha, 2013.

www.ingramcontent.com/pod-product-compliance
Lightning Source LLC
Chambersburg PA
CBHW021859230426
43671CB00006B/446